THE CULTIVATION OF I AM

A KNOW THYSELF CURRICULUM
THE BOOK OF HARDCORE REALITY

THE CULTIVATION OF I AM

A KNOW THYSELF CURRICULUM
THE BOOK OF HARDCORE REALITY

By Sheik Andrell Parham Bey©™

Self-Published with help from
MIDNIGHT EXPRESS BOOKS

THE CULTIVATION OF I AM

A KNOW THYSELF CURRICULUM
THE BOOK OF HARDCORE REALITY

ISBN-13: 978-0692396032 (Midnight Express Books)

ISBN-10: 0692396039

Self-Published with help from
MIDNIGHT EXPRESS BOOKS
PO Box 69
Berryville AR 72616
(870) 210-3772
MEBooks1@yahoo.com

THE CULTIVATION OF I AM

A KNOW THYSELF CURRICULUM
THE BOOK OF HARDCORE REALITY

By Sheik Andrell Parham Bey©™

ACKNOWLEDGMENTS

I rise and extend praise to THE ALL of All in manifest, namely ALLAH - the Divine Mentalism that corresponds Reality manifesting in vibrations of every frequency and sound throughout all Universes and beyond.

Honors and respects go to the Ancients for building the Mystery Schools and high degree education that equipped our Ancestors to construct civilization.

Honor and respect goes to Prophet Noble Drew Ali, for reconstructing the path to civilization, knowledge of self and the tools necessary to build Paradise/Heaven on earth, in Earth -via- the Divine and National Movement called the Moorish Science Temple of America, for those of us who were/are lost in the dark.

Honor and respect goes to prophets of ALLAH, namely: Jesus, Mohammed, Buddha, and Confucius. I also extend honors and respect to every branch and venue of the Moorish Nation, the Nation of ISLAM, the 5% Nation of Gods and Earths, the Afrikan Hebrew Israelites of Dugdumunuyah, Israel under Rabbi Ben Ammi, all Christian structures, Buddhists, all AL-ISLAM Muslims, Anthroposophists, Kemetic Scientists, the Fall Back Movement and all Honorable Masons of Ancient light and structure who are perpendicular to the Square and Ancestrial principles.

Special honor, respect, love and thanks goes to my Mother, Minister Anna Parham, my Auntie Gardenia Parham and my uncle, mentor and teacher, Frederick (Skeet) Parham. Without you three and all of the love, encouragement, support and assistance you extended, I could not, and would not have accomplished this portion of works.

To every righteous brother I've made contact with here in prison, who Comprehends and embraces the philosophy of my "Hardcore Realist" Character, I say thank you for building with me, helping me grow and Comprehend the significance of having an opened mind to learn from all sides. My gratitude to you all is unlimited.

DEDICATION

Ahlexis Andreya Parham and Aaryeana Jenae Parham, this Book of Hardcore Reality and its entire brand are dedicated to your generation and you. Learn it, discern it and then serve Humanity with it.

I love you both with everything I have.

Your Father and Uncle,

Dre

SPECIAL THANKS

This special thanks goes to my Parham family for never giving up on me, the School of Anthroposophy and the mentor assigned to me - Mrs. Mary Palmer, the Moorish Science Temple of America and the Grand Sheik of Subordinate Temple #5 - Kevin McLetchie El-Bey, the Fall Back Movement and its founder, Labron Neal Bey©™, for granting me the opportunity to manufacture the curricular base for the entire organization nationwide, and appointing me as the director of education for any educational ventures the organization may engage in or unite with.

Special thanks to Peter X, for helping me construct the Alphabet of Akh-Hulebuk, to Tommy Smith El©™, for proofreading this material, to Alfred Moore Bey©™, for helping to build the concept, to Andre Patterson for supplying the much needed data over the years of building, and all who extended assistance in the composing of this work, thank you all.

PREFACE

The Thinking Systems of many people today have been corrupted with all kinds of atrocious patterns of decision making. Reviewing the various conditions that have emerged from this atrocity, there's found selfishness, stupidity, ignorance, foolishness, perversion, misdirected anger, violence, racism and many other attributes stemming from this atrocious decision making of the people. It has come to the point where, such irresponsibility has been popularized into being the leading example of culture in this era and society.

Upon such careful analysis, it is legitimate to classify this leading example of derailed culture with a socio-diagnosis of being, "anti-social", "Mentally ill", and/or having an "attention deficit disorder" - in some cases with "hyperactivity" (ADD, ADHD). The behavioral dysfunctions emerging from this bad sense of decision making, stems from a misdirection of Thinking. As a consequence, up and coming generations of youth are falling into this distortion of culture, being preyed upon by the various corrupted opportunists. Anything that is lacking "order" is in utter "chaos." Reality holds that we who fall into any measures of chaos, are failing to protect our children and all youth at large. It is not the activity of Chaos that we should collectively try correcting; this is what your corrupted opportunist attack, which is seen in the art of prison building and packing, as the base solution, rather than building the equality and necessary mechanics to confront the various mental issues prevalent in the psyches of potential criminals; all statutory provisional writing, school closings, punishments of violence, mental, social or physical abuse, yelling, public humiliations and what have you, or the manufacturing of pharmaceutical drugs, chemicals and diagnosis catering to chaos. We can't expect any such brutality, business or politics to cure chaos. Chaos emerges from misdirected Thinking; and Thinking at this degree escapes the bounds of balance. Balance is order. Thus, correction in this manner comes from Reality, dealing in Reality as a Hardcore Realist, and all educational diagrams that manifest from this order. In other words, all behavioral dysfunctions which emerge from the chaos of bad decision making today, are learned and are calculated disorders, manufactured by corrupt opportunist of business structures for profit. The mis-education and its subliminal market of promotion benefits big business which is amalgamated into the corporate scheme of things. A balanced Thinking System of order will begin to "Real"-ize how, funeral homes, court buildings, jails, prisons, pharmacies, hospitals, police departments, attorneys, undertakers, public school boards and administrators, and news media, are the leading opportunists of a corrupted stature today.

Without the chaos of bad decision making amongst the people, none of these subordinate, incorporated and/or private business venues would be prime time infrastructures. These corporate industries would in fact, fall in upon themselves without the chaos of bad decision making. Just as chaos is learned, order must be learned. This is the beginning to Comprehending how to establish solution.

Epidemically, our children today are being picked off by the corrupted opportunists. Unbeknownst to their vulnerable and perplexed Thinking Systems, the profiting business venues of opportunity have estimated the future fillings of jails and prisons. They've determined how to criminalize the naive ones through the creations of new statutory laws. They've become better at marketing crime through entertainment, news media, and how to promote over-the-counter pharmaceutical drugs through commercial advertising. They've created sitcoms that show the business structure of incarceration, the legal system, shrewd politicians and what have you, continuing to breed separation, breaking up into classes, social disorder, broken families and hopelessness amongst a disoriented people.

Look around today! HIV/AIDS is prevalent in targeted communities. Incarceration and building the industrial stock is big business. Crime is extreme, statutory laws are legislated and made "tough on crime." Schools are being closed down to create gang violence amongst youth more broad, and no solution is being presented by us. I AM a Chicago native who fell victim to the destructive chaos of the 90's, and am now paying the ultimate price of incarceration as I AM 14 years into a 60 year sentence. Coming from the Morgan Park area on the South Side of Chicago during the wild 100's era of the 90's, I'm no backseat, inexperienced, analyst of Chaos. I've existed in a chaotic Thinking System and thrown away everything for what experience taught to be nothing. In Chicago right now, the same Thinking System of chaos has advanced into a more disturbing issue that we must work together to bring solution to. Remember that chaos and its activity is not what we should attack, nor try correcting. Chaos is learned and emerges from misdirection of Thinking. Our responsibility together, is to bring solutions to Thinking in balance.

This is not a book surrounding the pinpoints of what's wrong. We can all see from various perceptual angles the wrong of our collective circumstances. This is **"The Book of Hardcore Reality"**, and it surrounds the pinpoints of what's right. See, I can willingly admit to have once been a part of the problem who today, has worked extremely hard to be a part of the solution.

In truth, our children need our collective guidance, as they are being targeted for the next means of profiteering designed by corporate opportunists. I see today, in 2013, how schools in Chicago are on the brink of being closed down. As a part of the solution, I wanted to create the necessary basis for a Real Education. For it is a Real Education that will help us all come to grips with what chaos is, what order is, and how to Comprehend an order that can be brought out of chaos. Hence, this **B**ook of **H**ardcore **R**eality (**BHR**) will surround the pinpoints of what's right and what's Real.

I'm sure that we can all agree today that the public school curriculum is not designed to teach people about Reality or existence. The public school curriculum is in fact a multicultural paradigm set to promote the academic skills to deal in consumerisms, and the mercantile commercial world of trade.

I AM not saying that this structure of education is bad; I'm simply saying that this caliber education does not bring solution to what we agree our atrocious issues are. Our issues are—internal, and calls for mental and spiritual development. These issues are in our communities, classified as non-educational, and pushed into the jurisdictional venue of religion. The problems with religions of today that seemingly lack the qualification of producing any solution to the 'at hand' problems are: they are dogmatic, are of belief in worshipping ideas, and they lack the education stemming from nature and its workings.

These are the new-time religions that prevail today. I do not want to promote any religions of today as working solution to our 'at hand' problems. This is no knock on any religion or dogmatic belief. My intentions are to present an educational curriculum that reflects the ancient paradigms of Order, and do my part in making a Conscience contribution that is an accurate and workable solution to our problems. The ancients built their bases of curriculums in myths, because mythology was the masterful design that constructed the elementary teachings, advanced teachings and masterful teachings on/of the workings of the forces of nature. By way of mythology, the ancients crafted Mystery Schools and Sacred Halls of Learning, dealing in the forces of nature, magnetic and atomic energy of infinity and how The All of such Hardcore Reality interplayed on the solar system of the external Universe, and solar system of the internal You-niverse. The quality of teaching children this supreme order was established as **the Supreme** Intelligence of **S**cience, **L**aw, **A**rchitecture, and **M**athematics. Outcomes were extreme. **Our Ancient Ancestry was the Grand Orderly Divine Mothers and Fathers of civilization. They taught all comers to Know Thyself. "Religion" of this ancient venue was educational in the practice of building** Infrastructures - **S**ymbolism - Labors - **A**ncestry - and **M**orality; where the people were initiated into chambers that taught the link between Reality - the Light of the Word, and existence - nature and her laws. The Light of the Word is spiritual and considered in the beginners degree as the Sun/Son; and the means of the Sun/Son experiencing existence in flesh is through the mechanical building blocks of nature. Nature in the beginner's degree is considered the Mother. **Thus the "religion of Ancient," was the Knowledge of Self. We are in fact and truth the Light/Sun of Nature/The Mother. So, the ancient educational structure was Masonry - Ma -** Mother, **Son** = Sun/Light. **I-Self-Law-AM, Ma-son/Mason.** This is not "Free"-masonry, nor does this curriculum have anything at all to do with "Free"-masonry; its system, secrecy, oaths or modern idea of brother/sister-hood. This is no fraternal structure of education presented to you. The design of the curriculum is patterned from ancient ideas and means of establishing Hardcore Reality that brings resolve to all uncivilized, learned Thinking Systems of chaos. Also, I'd like to be clear in making known that "new time religious" ideas and/or dogma of any kind regarding ISLAM are in no way linked to this educational curriculum.

The ISLAM presented to the reader and Students of this curriculum are of ancient construction, and predates 13th Century Al-ISLAM. This is an educational platform that will enlighten all Students of ISLAM only being called ISLAM due to it being spelled out: Infinity - Sound - Light - Animation - Mentalism; Intelligence Science - Law - Architecture - Mathematics; Infrastructure - Symbolism - Labor - Ancestry - Morality. **This ISLAM is spelled out in activity of subject matters; and it is nothing that we submit to - I-Self-Law-AM ... The Master; ISLAM is who and what we are.**

As just a curriculum of Self Knowledge, this small Book of Hardcore Reality is titled: **The Cultivation of I AM**. To cultivate means to rise up and produce.

It is to apply self to improving and development. It is to form and redefine as by education. **I AM, is the Hardcore Reality of Spirit. It is** Intelligence of **A**ll **M**otion, Infallible **A**rchitect of **M**entalism, Inviolable Animator of **M**astery ... **It is The All of P**ure Infinite Energy. What I have tried to accomplish with this work, is to begin to raise up our people and produce a contribution that will help us all comprehend, that **we are the I**ntelligence of **A**ll **M**otion; We've put in major work that will help individuals apply themselves to improvement and developing into **the I**nfallible **A**rchitect of **M**entalism. I've designed a system that will form and refine our Thinking Systems into the education of Inviolable Animation of **M**astery. As our Ancient Ancestors rose up in degree into God-Consciousness and constructed civilizations, so shall we raise up in degree into God-Consciousness and re-construct civilization.

It is our responsibility to not try changing the arrangement of confusion and chaos designed by corporate orders of rule, but to rather educate ourselves to know how to protect our youth from the snares we couldn't see that ruined our potential in our youth. Truth be told, we don't need any outside venue's permission - be it religious, political or freemasonic, to teach ourselves Order and raise up our youth accordingly. The challenge for us at this Point is knowing how to put aside our opinionated, dogmatic beliefs for the sake of coming together to save our youth. This Book of Hardcore Reality was the select choice and style of teaching, to rid ourselves of any potential religious battles, arguments, disagreements, or fallings outs.

The Cultivation of I AM is only the myth that starts the process of working together. As an educational curriculum, there will be lessons, lesson books, and assignments following this work that will teach and instruct from every angle, how to stand square in every subject necessary, to arm and protect our children. This is Real. I chose "Chapter and Verse" format for the Book of Hardcore Reality, because such an ancient style gives us the ability to interpret order according to our perceptual standings, and guide in accord with words of order. Our lesson books will cover: cosmology, astrology, psychology, sociology, physiology, biology, ecology, mythology, art, linguistics, civics, law, architecture, carpentry, health and math - up to geometry, all in degree rising systems. **I AM the director of education in the Fall Back Movement and writer of its educational foundation, of which this Book of Hardcore Reality represents. The founder of the movement, Labron C. Neal Bey©™, started this movement with the intentions of protecting our youth from strategic, methodical attacks they have no mature idea exists as a threat to their well being. Our works together are extreme and sincere towards our cause.** As the head of the educational department, the staff of writers that I have in support of the cause is small. **The Fall Back Movement is an evolving organization designed to eliminate gangs, foolishness, crime and ignorance.** We have agreed, as its hardest workers and molders, the founder and I, to construct this educational venture from scratch. Our objective is to get the lost in Thought, to Fall Back from learned, redundant slave Activity and become adult Human Beings that are Hardcore and Real. The objective of this independent curriculum is to give solutions to Real issues. The process is kind of slow due to staff being so small. We are evolving daily though; and more brothers and sisters are coming to their senses, and being prepared to contribute to our cause of upliftment.

There is hope that you also, will participate in this contributory cause, that we may all grow together and prevent future failures. Your participation will build this brand up to a power that will provide our youth in Chicago and at large, with: solutions and qualified education preparing them for order in spite of public schools being closed down, prevent incarceration and murder, stop gangbanging, using and dealing drugs, stop promiscuity and disease, help prepare them to take their place among so called leadership and rule with Order, and never allow another to have their birthrights stolen by corporate thieves. This is a call to order. Many talk and never do anything solutionary. Many like to argue and point out what's wrong without any quality skill to lead into what's right. Many don't do anything about our issues. Many join the corrupted opportunists to profit off our ignorance, and many are in denial about the problem being active. I was once a part of the problem, but now I AM part of the solution. Let's work together and make this a successful venture that we can all say we accomplished together for ourselves and our children.

In conclusion, I openly request assistance in the continuation of building an educational curriculum and lesson format from scratch. The Fall Back Movement's educational department is opened for any who'd like to participate in this cause. I AM open to suggestions, comments, (good or bad), and participation from all who are outright tired of the downward spiral of falling into a seemingly bottomless grave. I'm just a humble Student and Hardcore Realist, willing to learn from all who are willing to teach. Make contact with me and let's work to reconstruct civilization. May Love, Truth, Peace, Freedom and Justice be the Principles that unite us as one.

Squarely Standing,

Andrell Jason Parham Bey©™

All Rights Reserved

THE FALL BACK PLAN

From: The Director of Education

We want to be clear regarding the meaning and purpose of the Fall Back Movement's educational venue. When we say "Fall", we are referring to a specific mental state that the majority have been trained, or conditioned to have, to lose its upright or erect position in the Intelligence of every individual. When we say "Back", we are referring to the Intelligent individual reverting to the counter direction in Thinking, reasoning, decision making and responding to the trained and conditioned mental state. We are a "Movement", meaning a change from one position to another. Hence, "The Fall Back Movement" is the Intelligence of all active individuals changing their mental state from a trained and conditioned state of ignorance and foolishness that brings imbalance to Thinking, reasoning, decision making and responding, into a balanced mental state of upright principle, vision, education and morale.

The Cultivation of I AM, is the Know Thyself curriculum that starts every individual off on the path of reverting back to our mental state of balance. There is no other means of raising up the Consciousness of Man than Reality. This educational venue intends to serve the participants of/in the Fall Back Movement with education in nature, national, spiritual and social Reality, with subject matters in Intelligence, Science, Law, Architecture and Mathematics. This is not a religion, a gang, or anything negative.

This is the Youniversity of Real Education that is all designed to teach you how to learn yourself and teach our youth to do the same. Support our cause as we contribute our portion of solution to you for the greater good of us all. Join the Fall Back Movement today and learn your way through the Book of Hardcore Reality.

Sheik Andrell J. Parham Bey©™

WHO ARE WE?

We are an inmate led movement/initiative aimed at combating the drug induced gang culture that is responsible for destroying the moral fabric of our communities.

It is our goal to convince criminals, gangbangers, drug dealers and other social deviants to withdraw from their criminal activity, take full responsibility for their actions and begin to work constructively with community leaders against violence.

We further request that pastors and community leaders oversee this initiative by working with ex-offenders and inmates participating in the Fall Back Movement.

We encourage dialogue between the two groups in order to curtail crime in our neighborhoods.

WHAT DO WE BELIEVE?

A great number of ex-offenders enter the system every day. Many of these people have changed their ways of Thinking and want to make a positive difference in society.

Many rehabilitated prisoners and reformed ex-offenders are interested in working with public officials and community leaders to bring positive change to our communities, but sadly, these individuals have been either overlooked, or written off, as being worthless by the public.

The street credibility that these ex-offenders carry is of extreme importance to the youth on the streets. With the help of community leaders, this valuable commodity can be used to promote positive behavior and encourage a more hopeful attitude among young people who may have otherwise taken a negative path.

OUR RECOMMENDATIONS

As a starting point, the Fall Back Movement and its supporters recommend several concrete steps to help stop violence:

1) All inmates that want to join in and participate with the Fall Back Movement and its service to our youth must renounce any and all affiliation with any gang or criminal organization as defined by the Illinois Department of Corrections, or any institutional departmental administrative rule in any state.

2) Prisoners must enroll in an educational program at their current facility or via mail, to sharpen all academic, social and mental skills and abilities that will be much needed in the mentoring and enlightening of our youth.

3) We ask that all inmates agree to the petitioning of legislators passing legislation that would require every parolee to participate in community service programs relevant in nature to the crime the parolee was convicted of, to show initiative to willingly display responsibility and participation in solutionary measures.

4) We ask that community leaders, ministers, and others become familiar with the gang recognition test that is offered by the Fall Back Movement.

5) We ask that community leaders meet with ex-offenders to address the issues of violence in our neighborhoods to constructively work

out solutions to our problems in a unified measure.

6)   We ask that every member exercise discipline, self-respect, respect for others and authority at large, and to always keep in Thought that you represent us, as we represent you. Your best behavior and decision making is required in all instances encountered.

Labron C. Neal Bey - G.S., D.M.

Table of Contents

"Man is to become God-like through a life of virtue, and the cultivation of the Spirit through Scientific knowledge, practice and bodily discipline."

-Ancient Egyptian Proverb

⑦

CHAPTER 1
The Beginnings of Order,
Chaos and Order Out of Chaos

1. In the incomprehensible realm of **P**ure **I**nfinity, there is an immeasurable, unreachable imminence of immortality. It is invisible to the calculations of materialism and deemed incorporeal, nothing and illusion.

2. In what seems to be an abode of immaterial Nothingness, there is Immortality that is Everything. The Everything of what seems to be an abode of nothing is the unknowable **Hardcore Reality of THE ALL**.

3. In the Nothingness that withholds Everything, there are no standings of calculated magnitudes. There is no space or time, or any source of things holding beginnings or endings. **Everything is THE ALL - An Immortal Living MIND of P**ure Infinity.

4. In this realm of Pure Infinity, Everything Is ALL; No partners, no records, because everything with records and partners has beginnings and endings.

5. **The expansion of THE ALL is Reality. No beginning or ending can determine Reality. Hardcore Reality is the Everything that forever lives as P**ure Infinite Energy; **the Spiritual MIND.**

6. **The Spiritual Reality of THE ALL is the unknowable, unmoveable, Great G**alactic-**O**mniscient **D**imension of **P**ure Infinity. It **is the unseen Actuality in Everything.**

7.   **The Great Galactic-Omniscient Dimension of Pure Infinity is The Everything of ALL Mentalism**. It is the Reality of all mental worlds.

8.   Everything is, always was, and will forevermore be in this Great Galactic- Omniscient Dimension. Everything images the Spiritual Mentalism of THE ALL, as this Great Galactic-Omniscient Dimension houses the Mental Hardcore Realism of Oneness.

9.   Within the Great Galactic-Omniscient Dimension, THE ALL opened the Mental Expansions of Everything for the energies of Hardcore Reality. From within those Great Infinite Heights of the Great Galactic-Omniscient Dimension came the Spiritual command for the energies of Hardcore Reality to reach the Great Infinite Depths. They poured out of the expansion with Oneness.

10.   **THE ALL uttered the word, "BE;" It traveled as Divine Spiritual Mentalism, being the ALL's Thought with Infinite Force. This WORD in Motion was the Light of Mentalism. This Force was Mighty and Indefinite in Motion.**

11.   Vibrations of the WORD traveled in infinite frequencies into the Consciousness of the energies of Hardcore Reality, spreading across and throughout Pure Infinity, translating the various ranges of uncalculated motions traveling as the Light of THE WORD.

12.   The energies of Hardcore Reality carried the Light of THE WORD through Pure Infinity as Pure Infinite Correspondence collectively translating It as the Infinite Source of Vibration in Motion.

13.   Through this Source of Vibration in Motion, a mental nature began to take form known as the Universe. The Mentalism of THE ALL was translated as Universe, due to the spiritual versatility of the vibrational

4

motions contractive and expansive tendencies.

14.   Uncalculated contractions and expansions of Vibration in motion produced an energy of spiritual chaos throughout the Mentalism of the Universe. It was an entity of disharmony within the motions of vibrations traveling without cause or meaning.

15.   And this chaos was Spiritual as it was a mixture of Light and Darkness traveling together in an uncalculated, disharmonizing motion. This chaos was neither bad nor good, as this dual partnership vibrated on a spiritual plane. Finite perceptions are the determiners of right and wrong, good and bad, righteous and evil.

16.   Energy is neither finite, bad or good. Every working of THE ALL is Infinite, and Divine. And such was the vibrations in motion that structured chaos throughout the Universe.

17.   The energies of both light and darkness were the spiritual chaos manifesting space and frequencies of primordial Consciousness, as they shined and shaded synchronistically.

18.   The light gave the various energies of Hardcore Reality meaning, while the dark left the energies to either transcend, ascend or descend without boundary.

19.   Within primordial Consciousness, infinitude became manifest as the spiritual designer of bounds for all that chaos left uncalculated and in disharmony.

20.   No Height or Depth went undersigned, from the moment infinitude ranged frequency and spiritual sound as bounds. From this, dimensions contracted and expanded, bringing about Length and Width.

21. Light still shined while darkness still dimmed at the same synchronistic measure, traveling without cause now, in Height, Depth, Length and Width, dimensionally.

22. **THE ALL seen that outside of Its realm of Pure Infinity, the expansion of Its Mentalism was uttered into Spiritual manifest. All spiritual energies working together in Oneness were the Energies of Hardcore Reality, throughout and within the Youniverse.**

23. This spiritual manifest formed a spiritual sound that carried the Pure Infinite Source of Vibration in Motion throughout Infinitudes dimensions of Height, Depth, Length and Width.

24. This spiritual sound became known throughout the Universe as the voice of the Great Galactic-Omniscient Dimension, and it was called the Great God of Infinity.

25. From the voice of the Great God of Infinity, Infinitude designed translations of sound in various spiritual forms throughout the Universe, extending into infinite Heights, Depths, Lengths and Widths dimensionally.

26. Within this 4 dimensional Reality, Universal Time measured the Spiritual workings as commanded by the voice of the Great God of Infinity; and this Force of Time became the ruling structure of the 4 dimensions. No finite time could measure the spiritual working of Hardcore Reality as Hardcore Reality is a part of Everything; and Everything is THE ALL - an Immortal Living Mind of Pure Infinite Energy.

27. Now the Universe of Mentalism was overflowing with the rich imminence of Pure Infinite Energy. It was due to the synchronology of

light and darkness that the Universe could hear the voice of the Great God of Infinity.

28. There was no good or evil; right or wrong, good or bad in their labors as they shined and dimmed at the same time with no structured cause. It was the labors of light and darkness, that helped infinitude manifest the sound of spiritual perfection and structured the Genesis of primordial Consciousness.

29. THE ALL was pleased; and it gave the Great God of Infinity Equilibrant Form and Authority to Rule the Universe of Mentalism.

30. And lo, The Great God of Infinity became the unmoved, incalculable, manifest Infinite Authority of THE ALL's Mentalism.

31. **Now as The Voice and Infinite Authority, the Great God of Infinity was known and recognized by all manifest spiritual energies of Hardcore Reality within the Mental Universe as ALL— AH (ALLAH) — The Supreme, Divine Ruler of the Mental Universe/Youniverse.**

32. **"THE ALL" is the Living Mind of Pure Infinite Energy. The "AH" is the representation of Corresponded Vibrations, known throughout the dimensions of the Mental Universe as the Voice of Spiritual Sound.**

33. **Hence, the Ruler of the Mental Universe was, is and forever more will BE, ALLAH.**

34. **And ALLAH spoke to the Universe of Mentalism: "I AM ... Pure Infinite Spirit—The Imminent, immeasurable Everything of what appears to be Nothing ... THE ALL of All throughout the**

Motions of Vibration. **My expansion is Hardcore Reality. The Spiritual Source of Time always was and forever will BE, having no start and no finish. For if a Beginning and Ending could ever BE in Spirit, I AM, the Beginning and the Ending.**

35. "All energies are manifest from my expansion; and ALL energies in the Mental Universe are Infinite—From The Light of Mentalism to Vibration in Motion, to chaos, to Infinitude and primordial Consciousness.

36. **"To All throughout My expansion of Hardcore Reality, I AM; the Great Universal** Intelligence of All Motion **in Spirit**; **I AM, the** Infallible Architect of Mentalism. **I AM the** Inviolable Animator of Mastery ... **ALLAH, The Ruler of the Mental Universe."**

37. All energies of spiritual manifest, submitted to ALLAH, the Great I AM's authority.

38. ALLAH gazed upon the expansions of the Universe; observing the workings of Light and Darkness and noticed them working together to be one, rather than working together as one.

39. And ALLAH spoke throughout the expansions: "As Mentalism is Corresponded in Vibrations, Poles of dimensions are formed in Rhythm of Light and Darkness' workings in one. With this, the Universal Mentalism expands and contracts without Cause. There must BE a Cause that structures Effects, that all things that manifest dimensionally may have purpose, meaning and a basis.

40. **"Purpose must define Vibration in Motion. Without Purpose, All Spiritual Traveling has no meaning; Purpose is the basis of cause that structures effects; without it, the Traveling of Vibration**

to every frequency has no meaning. Anything without meaning is not in Balance.

41.   "Balance is the Order of Motion; it is the establisher of Purpose, meaning and a basis. Without these, there is no Purpose; and without purpose, there is no balance. Where there is no balance, there's chaos - motion with no bounds.

42.   "In the expansion of Everything, the energies of Hardcore Reality begets boundless things; things are in utter chaos. Chaos is a wondrous working of the energies of Hardcore Reality; being a team of light and darkness working synchronistically with no agreement on balance.

43.   "Infinitude is the architect of design that gives this wondrous working frequency. This is Chaos in Order; and as long as this stands, order will never be structured. Boundlessness must be stabilized with boundaries of balance.

44.   "Thus, let Infinitude BE clothed in aggregate cosmic garb, that Chaos in Order may BE constructed into THE ORDER THAT COMES OUT OF CHAOS. Then let Us have Chaos on one hand and Order on the other."

45.   Obeying the command of ALLAH, The Great I AM, Infinitude took on cosmic garb and brought a design to the Universe with Galaxies, Ozones, Dimensions, Stars and elements. And of these manifest workings, Genders formed to advance their position.

46.   A separation of Light and Darkness became manifest. Both Light and Darkness became two separate entities in the spiritual world of infinity.

47.   Darkness without the Light became the stillness of the Universe and polarity of motion. Light became the motion of Mentalism throughout the Universe/Youniverse.

48.   Now separated from joint existence, both Light and Darkness had Purpose; they worked together in Balance, harmonizing to bring meaning to color.

49.   As Infinitude took on cosmic garb, Gender was given to the dual partnership that worked together in Balance. The Light was given male gender, as it was an expanding Force that penetrates Darkness, which was given female gender that contracted.

50.   Working together in Balance, Light was now Born through Darkness; it was because of Spiritual Darkness that Light became visible in colors.

51.   With divine Purpose, Darkness became the Spiritual Womb of the Mental Universe, and Light became Animate Motion manifest through this Cosmic Womb. And this working of Balance was called Order.

52.   When Light and Darkness are In disharmony - working outside of Cause and Divine Purpose, while trying to be one at the same time, this erases bounds, disrupts Order and is called Chaos.

53.   ALLAH, The Great I AM, commanded the establishment of Order to come from Chaos, and bring all motion into the Divine Purpose.

54.   Infinitude obeyed the command of ALLAH, The Great I AM and constructed Spiritual Separation of establishments. There was now Chaos in Order as an establishment of boundless Motion without Cause called

CHAOS, and there was An Order constructed out of Chaos as an establishment of Light, manifesting through the Womb of Darkness with Divine Purpose called ORDER.

55.   After all was established, ALLAH, The Great I AM, beheld the cosmic garb that manifest as the Light of the WORD through the Cosmic Womb of Darkness, and manifested as the attributed Source of Light within the garb of Spiritual Fire.

56.   **This Infinite Spiritual establishment of Order throughout the Mental Universe was called: Intelligence; Pure Infinite Energy of Hardcore Reality corresponded with Infinitude, in Vibrational Motions that ranged in frequencies of Genius, Excellence, Navigation, Consciousness and Evolution.**

57.   Now ALLAH, the Center Source of Intelligent Animate Motion, was the Light of The WORD in the Universe of Mentalism, while Darkness was the Womb of the Universe of Mentalism. In this established constructed order, ALLAH, The Great I AM was the Father of The Universe of Mentalism and Darkness was the Matrix called "Ma", or "Mother."

58.   ALLAH said: "Infinitude of the Universe, I AM ALLAH, the Great I AM, Father of the Universe. The Womb of the Universe through which I penetrate with Light is the Mother.

59.   "You are the Council through which I, The Great I AM, extend Divine Authority to, as the Council of Spiritual Order. I give all Supreme Authority to Create in this Order, and Define All that you Create.

60.   "I AM, the Pure Infinite Source of your Supreme **G**enerating-**O**perating-**D**istributing **Power**, as I center my Supreme Force within the

Light of the Spiritual Fire around which you encompass, that Balance may define the basis of All Motion.

61.   "Your Authority is Supreme and Divine, as this Council is the Grand Celestial Spiritual Body Magnifying Order out of Chaos.

62.   "The Supreme Grand Body of Power is henceforth, **the Grand Order of Divine Service - The Governing Council of GODS,** and will BE recognized throughout the contractions and expansion of Everything as the Creator of Manifest Order in Motion"

63.   The Governing Council of GODS formed themselves into Government of Order, spreading the Order in Rhythmic Motion throughout the Infinity of the Universe/Youniverse.

64.   Every **G**alaxy, **O**zone, **D**imension and **S**tar took the Governmental form of Order, encompassing the Pure Infinite Source of **G**enerating-**O**perating-**D**istributing **Power** that was the Light of the Spiritual Fire. And there was subsequent praise extended to Father ALLAH - The Great I AM in the harmony of Cosmic Song that was only comprehended by the Father, Mother and cosmic hosts.

65.   With this God Power of Authority, the Spiritual Council of GODS called for Equilibrant Form to become manifest through every measurement dimensionally, and in every Galaxy, Ozone and Star that came from the Cosmic Dark Matter of The Womb of the Universe and the Pure Infinite Light of ALLAH, The Great I AM.

66.   And it became the "First Spiritual Rule of Order" set forth by the Council of GODS, for All cosmic hosts in every dimensional measurement, galaxy, ozone, star, and aggregate element to: Honor the Infinite Father and Mother - ALLAH, The Great I AM and Ruler of the

Universe, and the Universal Cosmic Womb of Dark Matter through which All Light Evolves and Shines.

67. Throughout the expansions of **All G**alaxies, ozones and dimensional **measurements**, the Council of GODS formulated Rules of Order that maintained Balance. And the Rules were Spiritually documented in **The Order of** Infinite Sounds of Light Animating Mentalisms **Motions**.

68. **Within the Spiritual Motion of** Infinity, Sound, Light, Animation and Mentalism, **all cosmic hosts that were the Light/Sun/Son of Dark Matter the Universal Mother, took the document of Spiritual Rules Formulas of Order, and designed Universal Equations of** Intelligence, Science, Law, Architecture and Mathematics.

69. These Spiritual Universal Equations became the building blocks to portals that manifested Mathematical openings to Mental Worlds, where Time became a part of Space and Mass in degree dimensional measurements of Equational Solution. And these Equational Solutions represented the Mentalism of the Cosmic Womb of the Universe and ALLAH The Great I AM, to create an Intelligent, Scientific, Lawful, Architectural, Mathematical record of events.

70. The Suns/Sons/Lights that created worlds in the 4 dimensional measurements of Height, Depth, Length and Width, calculated Spiritual Time as the Balance between Light and Dark Matter while outside of the 4 dimensional measurements, Time had no bearing on the Spiritual Present Moment.

71. In the dimensional measurement of Height, Depth, Length and Width, every degree from every measured angle was set in Balance around the Spiritual Structures of Consciousness of the Present Moment.

72. Spiritual Tools were manufactured that All Building Blocks Mathematical Openings, could be created with balanced design around the Consciousness of the Present Moment.

73. Within this measurement, time was given the Authoritative position of structuring the Pole for the Spiritual Present Moment's Balance in Height, Depth, Length and Width for the Cosmic Mentalism of Equational Solutions Building Blocks in Intelligence, Science, Law, Architecture and Mathematics.

74. Furthering the Cause of Formulated Rule by the Council of GODS, these Suns/Sons/Lights of Dark Matter - the Universal Cosmic Mother and Father ALLAH, The Great I AM, took the Spiritual Tools and Built Cosmic Mansions of Mentalism, to House/Shelter the Cosmic Equational Solutions, stemming from the Council of GODS Formulated Rule.

75. The Council of GODS seen the workings of the cosmic hosts, admiring the labors. They amalgamated into the consciousness of the Present Moment's measurements, utilizing the Spiritual Tools to build a Governing Panel around Time's Authoritative position.

76. Around the structure of Time and Balance of the Pole within the Consciousness of the Present Moment, the Council of GODS calculated into the Spiritual Equation, foundations for Cosmic Government.

77. And it was declared by the Council of GODS that within the dimensional measurements of the Equational Solutions, structure of Time and Balance on the Pole within the Consciousness of the Present Moment, where the Cosmic Mansions of Mentalism reside, Intelligence, Science, Law, Architecture and Mathematics would be the structure and Principle of every Measured Angle in the Circumference of the Area.

78. The circumference of the Area was called "Faluizzi•", which meant the Authoritative Cosmic Order of Time, structured in the Zodiac Mansions of Mentalism in the Universe.

79. The Council of GODS were calculated as 9. They were 9 Grand Governors granted Authority to Create and Define by Father ALLAH, The Great I AM; Ruler of the Mental Universe.

80. In Faluizzi, they Governed the workings of the cosmic hosts in 7 seats: called the 7 Eyes of ALLAH.

81. The Council of GODS, in Faluizzi, were Judges Governing the Mental Structure of Order. They were 9 Grand Governors stationed in 7 seats surrounding the Mansions of Mentalism.

82. The 9 Grand Governors were named on the like: The first was Shaheh•; and was the Judge of ALLAH the Great I AM's Hardcore Reality.

83. The second was Shubu•; and was the Judge of Conscious Navigation; the 3rd was Shahra•; and was the Judge of Animate Governing;

84. The 4th was Shleyah•; and was the Judge of Evolution in Intelligence, Science, Law, Architecture and Mathematics; the 5th was Shkeduh•; and was the Judge of Mentalism and Knowledge;

85. The 6th was Shebuk•; and was the Judge of Love and Principle of every measured Angle in the circumference of the Area; the 7th was Shfahu•; and was the Judge of Order and Chaos in every working and arrangement;

86. The 8th was Shlebu•; and was the Judge of Evolutionary Navigation and the 9th was Shmumah•; the Judge of Degrees of Wisdom.

87. Through them, a Spiritual Master's Key was formed that both locked and unlocked portals outside of Faluizzi.

88. And ALLAH, the Great I AM spoke to the Council of GODS and said unto them: "Through this Master's Key, you nine Grand Governors Judge All stations within Reality. The Doors to Pure Infinity can always be opened by you; and the 2 doors on the dimensional measurements Spiritual Structures of Consciousness of the Present Moment, every degree you can open.

89. "Outside of our Infinite Realm of Hardcore Reality, your Infinite Authority over All things by the Creative WORD, can and must design equilibrant form with the consciousness of the Present Moment as the basis.

90. "Continue to Build through the cosmic hosts, the equations that make up the Order of Intelligence, Science, Law, Architecture and Mathematics, that All solutions to every degree may bring honor to your Govern - Mental Panel.

91. "And I, Father ALLAH, the Great I AM, will Be the Spiritual Motion of vision through your 7 Eyes. The 1st Eye and seat will be Bazibu; this is the seat of Shaheh, the 1st Judge. This seat is the Head of the Council, and Giver of Life.

92. "The 2nd Eye will BE Kefabu; this is the seat of Shhubu, the 2nd Judge. This seat is the Giver of Emotion, Instinct and Desire. The 3rd Eye will BE Luzile; this is the seat of the 3rd Judge, Shahra; and is the Giver of Zeal and Manifest Activity in all Elements of Equational

Solution in Faluizzi.

93. "The 4th Eye will BE Mahlemu; this is the seat of the 4th and 8th Judges, Shleyah and Shlebu: this Seat is the Giver of Intellect, Reason, Logic, Social Balance, Growth, change, original vision and the ability to make acute decisions. The 5th Eye will BE Luehzileh; this is the Seat of Shkeduh, the 5th Judge and is the Giver of Expansive Knowledge and transdimensional perception.

94. "The 6th Eye will BE Akhleyah; this is the Seat of both Shehbuk; and Shmumah; the 6th and 9th Judges and is the Giver of Love, Natural Law, expression of Love, inspiration, ideology, Universal Morale and standings on things that are Natural; the 7th Eye will be Baahlu; this is the seat of Shfahu; the 7th Judge and is the giver of Discipline, Direction, Order, Chaos, or both.

95. "Open up the estate to God Dominion throughout your Arranged Equations high degree Solutions, that the Solutions in Formula may manifest as **Infinite-Divine-Dual** entities of Light and Darkness in Faluizzi, that must Travel the planes to experience your exhibited execution of God Power angled through my 7 Eyes, in the Consciousness of the Present Moment.

96. "From my 7 eyes, let the 7 Sources of Equational Solution contract and expand through the Womb of Cosmic Dark Matter, into the Rhythmic Motion of the Mansions Mental Wheel of Motion Set by Time.

97. "In Times Authoritative measurement, I grant the Spirit of Pure Infinite Energy the Traveling Luxury of Being the Light of Motion in Faluizz.:"

98. From the 7 Eyes of ALLAH, the Great I AM, All Motion

contracted and expanded in and through the Cosmic Womb of Dark Matter, into the manifest 7 sources of Equational Solution.

99.   **As the Wheel of Mansions moved in a Rhythmic Order within the Divine Focus of The 7 Eyes of ALLAH, The Great I AM, 7 Universal stages emerged that gave the 7 Sources of Equational Solution the ability to manifest in Mass Aggregate form. And the 7 Universal Stages were a Ladder that the 7 Sources of Equational Solution had to climb in Faluizzi. They were: 1. Nature, 2. Ether, 3. Astral, 4. Soul/ego, 5. Subtle, 6. Causal, 7. ALLAH, The Great I AM.**

100.   **And the Mass aggregational formation of the 7 Sources of Equational Solution were called: Proton, Neutron, Electron, Weak Force, Strong Force, Electromagnetism and Gravity.**

101.   The Council of GODS obeyed ALLAH The Great I AM, and utilized the Spiritual Tools In concert with the 7 Sources of Equational Solution, that had to climb the Universal Ladder of 7 Stages, to begin the working of Building an Evolutionary Vehicle for the Infinite - Divine - Duality of Light and Darkness to function in the Authoritative Measurements of Time in the Consciousness of the Present Moment.

102.   **The Infinite, Divine Duality of Light and Darkness was to be the Ruler of the Evolutionary Vehicle when it was complete. This Ruler was named:** Mentalism-Animating-Navigation/**MAN.**

103.   **And the Council of GODS said unto MAN: "Oh MAN, you are the Infinite - Divine - Duality of Light and Darkness that will manifest as Spirit into the Aggregations of Mass. You are Suns/Sons/Lights of ALLAH, The Great I AM and Universal Dark Matter.**

104.   "As you transition into your Mass Measurements, the Fire of Atom, and Nourishment of Evolution will give you structure. You are vested with the God Power of the Council of GODS.

105.   "From the Wheel of Mansions, your Infinite - Divine - Dual Spirit will amalgamate with Mass; and you, as Ruler of the Station, will Evolve as Atom in the measurement of Faluizzi, to establish Order out of Chaos in the Intelligence of Science, Law, Architectural, Mathematical Equational Order of degrees.

106.   "Of this Pure Infinite expansion, Dark Matter in the Cosmic Womb of the Universe is your Mother. ALLAH The Great I AM, Ruler of the Universe is your Father and we - the Council of GODS, seen through the 7 Eyes of ALLAH The Great I AM, are the Supreme Grand Governors and Cosmic Judges in Government who give Infinite Sounds, in signs of Light - Animating All Motions of Mentalism.

107.   **"Hence, you oh MAN, are the Cosmic National, that will Rule All Mass in Faluizzi as Spiritual Sovereigns. This is your Right of Evolutionary Birth into All that's Natural."**

108.   After being Raised up by Atom and Evolution, a Natural Mother will Nurture your Development in Mass as Spirit. Her name is called "Nuhfamuoh•".

109.   "And lo, you will leave the Sacred Halls of Learning in the Wheel of Mansions, be Raised up by Atom and Evolution and make a transition into the Nourishing Arms of Nuhfamuoh in a Calculated Order of Time, Conscious of the Present Moment.

110.   **"She shall be your Mother and she will call you as MAN, "Kebuk•" which means the Sun/Light/Son of the Mother, or Ma-**

Son.

111. **"The Power of your Birth Right comes with the charge of evolving from the Natural Law of your Natural Mother, to create and Define the Grand** Government **Of** Dominion **for yourself, and a Council, as it resides throughout the** Pure Infinite **expansions of your Cosmic Spiritual Home.**

112. "Contribute to the Health and Wealth of your Natural Mother, that she may say: "Ma-son/Kebuk, you have the Divine Vision of your Father, ALLAH The Great I AM, Ruler of the Universe.

113. "Bring Rhythmic Balance to your Natural Mother with the Governmental design of Intelligence, Science, Law, Architecture, Mathematics, as **you are a Cosmic National who will Rule the Natural.**

114. **"In Nuhfamuoh - Declare your National Name in** Intelligent, Science-of-Law, Architecture and Mathematics, **that will make you as Kebuk/Ma-son, have Natural Purpose in Evolutionary Development, through the Consciousness of The Present Moment.**

115. "In the Natural, Beginning and Ending will Become and Befall you. The Vehicle of Nuhfamuoh; is a slower Vibrational Sound, projected into Faluizzi - for only a Time measurement. **MAN must Raise up to Master, and Proclaim: I AM**; Nature is the first step towards that cause. Hence, there is Purpose, Basis and meaning to the Vehicle having a Beginning and an Ending.

116. "Fear it not; it is only a Support of your Natural position.

117. "And thus, you oh MAN who will become Ma-Son/Kebuk -

vested by the **Pure** Infinite **Order of ISLAM**, are the Creator, Ruler, Governor and National GOD that will Develop in a Natural Station in Faluizzi;

118. "We give you the Consciousness of this Council of GODS that you may go through the Sacred Halls of Learning in the Wheel of Mansions, be Raised up by Atom and Evolution and become a living Soul that will be Conscious in the Present Moment as Kebuk/Ma-Son."

119. And Order was brought out of Chaos, and handed to the **M**entalism-**A**nimating-**N**avigation that will become a living Soul in the Consciousness of the Present Moment and known in the Natural Plane as Kebuk/Ma-Son.

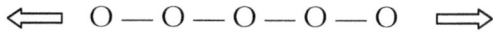

$$\Longleftarrow \quad O - O - O - O - O \quad \Longrightarrow$$

CHAPTER II
The Workings of Atom and Evolution in Faluizzi and Nuhfamuoh

1. In the expansion of the Universe, the Council of GODS moved through the Mansions in Rhythmic Motion structured by the Authoritative measurement of time. From their Rhythmic Motion into the Wheel, 12 Gates became manifest around the 12 Mansions.

2. Energies were stationed in each mansion, forming 12 vital qualities for the Infinite - Divine - Duality that was to become a living soul.

3. For the 12 vital qualities to Develop, their circle of labors was divided into four 90° Quadrants, each withholding a Team of three laborers.

4. It was the labors of forming the vehicle that the Spiritual Mentalism - Animating - Navigation will inhabit in the Consciousness of the Present Moment through Nuhfamuoh, the Natural Mother.

5. The workings of the Light of The WORD created the Sacred Halls of Learning in the mansions. that Developed the entry and exit Gates into the Authoritative Measurement of Time.

6. The First Team of Mansions was the 1st Mansion; 5th Mansion; and 9th Mansion; and these were the Spiritual Mechanics of Fire. Together they Built the Sacred Halls of Learning Knowledge, Energy and

Creativity; these 3 reached in the Spiritual Fire and pulled these Sacred Halls of Learning out in a School of 90°.

7.   The Second Team of Mansions was the 2nd Mansion, 6th Mansion and 10th Mansion; and these were the Spiritual Mechanics of Land. Together they Built the Sacred Halls of Learning how to acquire Personal Property, become Employed and Build Careers while utilizing the Spiritual tools. These 3 reached in the Spiritual expansion and pulled these Sacred Halls of Learning out in a School of 90°.

8.   And the 1st and 2nd Teams of Mansions together, all spun in a 180° Motion, Structuring their 6 Gates in a Masculine Order.

9.   The First and Second Teams 6 Gates in 180°, had The Sacred Halls of Learning that Structured the Energy to Create, and Learn how to Learn the Knowledge of Order to Build Personal Property and Employment as Careers with the Tools for All Masculine Principles to flourish in Nuhfamuoh. This Masculine gift was given to Atom, making him Male.

10. The Third Team of Mansions was the 3rd Mansion, the 7th Mansion and the 11th Mansion; and these were the Spiritual Mechanics of Air. Together they built the Sacred Halls of Learning how to deal in Family Units, with Relatives, deal in Partnerships that create Units and how to be and treat Friends with Friendship. These 3 reached, in the Spiritual Winds and pulled out the Sacred Halls of Learning in a School of 90°.

11. The Fourth Team of Mansions was the 4th Mansion, the 8th Mansion and the 12th Mansion; and these were the Spiritual Mechanics of Water. Together they built the Sacred Halls of Learning how to Prepare for Future endeavors, deal with the Natural transition of forms (death) and the Regeneration of Order through the Spiritual Insight. These 3

reached in the Spiritual Fluids and pulled out these Sacred Halls of Learning in a School of 90°.

12.   And the Third and Fourth Teams of Mansions together all spun in a 180° Motion, structuring their 6 Gates in a Feminine Order.

13.   The Third and Fourth Teams 6 Gates in a 180°, had the Sacred Halls of Learning that Structured Family Orientations through the Union of Partnerships with the First and Second Teams 180° Motion and 6 Gates, and Formulate Friendships that are sustained through latter years until the transition of Natural form occurs, and the meetings of Regeneration becomes spiritual in Nuhfamuoh. This Feminine gift was given to Evolution, making her Female.

14.   The Fire and expansion of Mass was within Atom the Male, to produce the Seed withholding the Source of Life to establish the means of Wealth.

15.   The Holy Breath of the winds intertwined with the Spiritual Fluids was within Evolution the Female, to conceive the Source of Life, condition it to its Relations and Duties upon producing it within the Consciousness of the Present Moment, and prepare it to Comprehend Beginnings, Endings and Pure Infinity.

16.   The 180° spin of the Masculine Principle and the 180° spin of the Feminine Principle, conjoined in Cosmic Harmony through their opposite Motions, that their Sacred Halls of Learning would become One Source.

17.   Throughout the expansions and contractions of Faluizzi, this 360° Creation of the Council of GODS through the Four 90° Quadrants and three Mansions within every 90° Break, was the 12 Gates of Masculine

and Feminine Principle called: the 360° Circle of Life; The Clock of Male and Female Destiny in Nuhfamuoh.

18.   **It was the 360° Circle, broken down into 4 Teams of 3 Mansions that manifested the Symbolic Number of Perfection in God-Consciousness that was 7.**

19.   **And 7 in this Circle became the Symbol of Perfection and Completion; the Circled 7; the Circle of Fire, Land, Air and Water.**

20.   Through the 12 Mansions within the Circled 7, Atom and Evolution were Educated in the Sacred Halls of Learning, passing through the 12 Gates into Nuhfamuoh• on an Angle of Light.

21.   As a 360° Function of Fire/Light and Air/Holy Breath, Land/Expansion of Mass and Water/Contraction of Spiritual Fluids, Atom and Evolution came to know one another in/through the Bonds of Affection.

22.   From Causal to Subtle form, they began to slowly transcend into a miniature Solar System, developing into a Microcosm that gave Nuhfamuoh• a pulse.

23.   Comprehending that they were 2 opposite ends of a Pole, they Raised Up Nuhfamuoh• and met in the Balance as Man. In times' Authoritative measurements, they developed in Vibrational Rhythm that manifested the Cause of the Council of GODS in their Dual Genders of Male and Female.

24.   Atom became the Husband and Balance of Hot and Cold and Evolution, his Wife, the Balance of Wet and Dry. And from their Divine Union, they gave birth to 12 children in Nuhfamuoh.

25.   And they were: 1. Oxygen, 2. Carbon, 3. Hydrogen, 4. Nitrogen, 5. Calcium, 6. Phosphorus, 7. Chlorine, 8. Sulfur, 9. Sodium, 10. Magnesium, 11. Iodine and 12, Iron.

26.   Through the Spiritual Generating - Operating - Distributing Power of the Council of GODS, every 90° Quadrants Break in the Clock of Male and Female Destiny, formed Seasonal Cycles of Hot, Cold, Wet and Dry.

27.   These cycles became spans of time through which the Children of Atom and Evolution Developed.

28.   The Circle of Life Seasonally Spun until the Energies of Light manufactured a Mass that Orbited in the gravitational pull of the Electromagnetic field of Nuhfamuoh, giving the Children of Atom and Evolution a Calculated Motion.

29.   And the Children of Atom and Evolution had children that had children that conceived and gave Birth to Twins. And they were called: Organic and Inorganic Compounds.

30.   **Through the Workings of these Two Sons, a Nature began to form that manifest from Soul, Astral and Etheric stages, constructing particles consisting of Atom's Seed, held together by Chemical bonds of Evolutionary design, constructing living organisms having dense central bodies, that holds genetic material.**

31.   **Just as it was in the Balance of Atom and Evolution's Union, the Council of GODS called this forming Nature: Man =** Molecular - **A**utonomical - **N**ucleus.

32.   As this Nature of Man Developed, the **Soul of Mentalism** -

Animating - Navigation **[Soul-of-MAN/Sol-O-Mon]** amalgamated into it as the Consciousness of the Present Moment, making the Nature of Man a transcendental vehicle in Nuhfamuoh.

33. From that moment a Full Spin on the Clock of Male and Female Destiny became manifest. Hundreds of Millions of Males and Females Developed through the Root of Atom and Evolution.

34. This Natural Man was the Supreme Working of Atom and Evolution's manifest generations offspring. The upright male and female Man of Natural Manifest in conjunction with the Spiritual Man—through its transcendental Vehicle, was named by Atom and Evolution, "Solomon," in the manifestation of the Order and Solomon, the hundreds of millions of males and females developed through the root of Atom and Evolution, was **fully capable of manifesting the basis of Hardcore Reality, by traveling the course of** Infinity - Sound - Light - Animation and Mentalism **through the Consciousness of the Present Moment.**

35. As Solomon developed in Nuhfamuoh, so did the Natural Nutritious substances, the Trees, Great Bodies of Water and the grounds. It was these things that Solomon learned to utilize for survival.

36. Staying active in Solomon's development, both Atom and Evolution stayed in the Subtle form. They were recognized by All developed generations as the Mother and Father of Man's Natural Development, and took All Souls through their Sacred Halls of Learning.

⇐ O — O — O — O — O ⇒

CHAPTER III
The Council of Gods Works the Variables in the Equational Solution and Builds Hotep

1. The Circle of Life Spun 3 times; and Solomon developed in Slow stages.

2. More attuned to Spiritual Order of Hardcore Reality, Solomon intently avoided the Natural Order by stepping out of Balance on the Pole and into ranges of vibrational frequency unseen and unheard in the Natural Plane.

3. There was an Awareness of the Hardcore Reality of Order being connected to the transcendental Vehicle, but no zeal to manifest the basis of Hardcore Reality in Nuhfamuoh.

4. The Council of GODS seen that there was a disharmony in Solomon's structure; the Natural Molecular Autonomical - Nucleus was not in Balance with the Spiritual Mentalism - Animating - Navigation. The Council of GODS knew that Solomon would not Master Times Authoritative Measurements, or contribute to Nuhfamuoh in such a stagnant disharmony.

5. And the Head of the Panel of the Council of GODS said unto The Council at large: "The Equational Solution has been calculated to

Become Microcosmic **Generators** - **O**perators - and - **Distributors of Light, contributing the Order of** Intelligence - Science - Law - Architecture - and - **Mathematics into the measurements of Time**.

6. "Solomon is The Balance of the Universal Ladder; the Soul-of-MAN within the transcendental Vehicle of Consciousness, traveling within the Natural Man's perception of the Present Moment. The Purpose of Solomon's reign in Order is to Learn the Treasures and Riches of Nuhfamuoh's Formula, that the productivity of **Intelligence** - Science - **Law** - **Architecture** - and - **Mathematics may unfold as the manifest** Infrastructures - of - **Symbolism** - **Labors** - of - **Ancestry's** - Morality **of Nuhfamuoh's Standings**.

7. "Upon realizing such facts, there comes the obvious necessity for Mathematical analysis. There are Variables of this Equational Structure that has yet to be solved.

8. "Solomon climbs the Universal Ladder from the Balance up into the **Hardcore Reality of the** Intelligence of **All Motion**; there are harmonious Connections; but when climbing down into the first Stair of Nature, Solomon won't unfold the Natural Basis.

9. "That which is Spiritual must harmonize with that which is Natural for ISLAM to unfold as Order.

10. "Hence let Us go down into Nuhfamuoh to assist Solomon into the Balance of God Power, that Time's measurements may be Mastered, and Nuhfamuoh be Built up into Order.

11. "We will show Solomon how to climb down the Universal Ladder and utilize Spiritual Equational Thought into the manifestation of Natural Order to begin the establishment of ISLAM."

12. And the Council of GODS ordained attributes of their Spiritual Energies to pass through all of the Sacred Halls of Learning in All 12 Mansions.

13. They passed through the 12 Gates and Traveled on an Angle of Light down the Universal Ladder into the Natural of Nuhfamuoh, to begin the process of Solomon's Mastery of Time and Rulership in Nuhfamuoh.

14. They took for themselves the transcendental garb and taught through the Male and Female Principles, the qualities of Gaining - Obtaining - Developing Order in the Present Moment.

15. Solomon began to unfold Responsive Comprehension in and of the Natural Order; from such became the Ruler of All that Was Natural. Tools were manufactured, clothes were tailored, food was stocked, the dead were properly managed and the animals were named.

16. And Solomon designed an Operative Guild of Shelter Builders that Built up the living stations in Nuhfamuoh. They were taught a Simplistic means of communicating and taught the Mastery of Utilizing every Tool in their trade. This Guild of Shelter Builders, Solomon called **Akh-Hulebuk•**.

17. After a full cycle of Seasons, the Council of GODS departed Nuhfamuoh and left Solomon as the Ruler and decision maker of Nuhfamuoh.

18. Akh-Hulebuk surrounded Solomon and Learned the many Subject Structures of **I**ntelligence - **S**cience - **L**aw - **A**rchitecture - and **M**athematics. They marveled at the visions told to them of One to come from Solomon's Seed, to Teach a Divine Service with the Workings of

the Tools beyond current Comprehension, that Will Build up Nuhfamuoh into Supreme Order.

19. Through the Guild called Akh-Hulebuk, Solomon expanded Wealth and Treasure throughout the Natural Plane, constructing the beginnings to Order out of Chaos.

20. And Solomon Ruled Nuhfamuoh with the Consciousness taught by the Council of GODS. Nuhfamuoh was blessed with the manifestation of Spiritual Tools in the Natural, the mechanics of upright formation, the Akh-Hulebuk Guild of Shelter Builders and the Supreme Wisdom of Solomon.

21. After the Variable unfolded the partition of Solomon's accomplishment in Nuhfamuoh, the Equation was considered to be partially Solved. The Circle of Life spun 3 times, and Solomon was summoned by the Council to take the Station on the 4th bar of Balance on the Universal Ladder.

22. Looking back into Nuhfamuoh, the Council of GODS seen that their labors in variable with Man in Nuhfamuoh were productive. For Akh-Huelbuk were the reigning line of Solomon's descendants.

23. And the Head of the Panel of Gods said unto the Council: "Lo we have served the Natural Molecular - Autonomical - Nucleus well. Solomon reigns Supreme through the Guild of Shelter Builders. Akh-Hulebuk has been Raised up to Be the Most Intelligent Scientist of Law, Architecture and Mathematics in Nuhfamuoh.

24. "We have Lawfully and Mathematically Solved one of the Variables to this Equational Solution. We've shown Solomon how to manufacture Spiritual Equational Thought into the manifest of Natural Order, and

Elevated this stair back into the Balance of the Universal Ladder. Akh-Hulebuk now has the foundational blueprint for Building up Nuhfamuoh With Solomon's perception of Hardcore Reality.

25. "Now then, let us behold the next variable of this Spiritual Equation, that the Natural Man's Gaining - Obtaining - Developing Consciousness in the Present moment may be Solved, and Man can define the manifest of Purpose Meaning and basis of Hardcore Reality.

26. "Solomon has well prepared Akh-Hulebuk to Learn, Discern and Serve the Spiritual Order of Hardcore Reality. Through this Seed they will be Taught **The Divine Evolution into G**overnmental **O**rder of **D**ivine **Power in Nuhfamuoh as Kebuk/Ma-Son**.

27. "In reverence to Atom's Learning Halls and Evolution's Mothership, Akh- Hulebuk must be Raised up into Learning to Discern the Spiritual Significance of the Light of the WORD in a Masters degree, that All Character may Comprehend the Supreme Circumstances of the Station of Service in the Intelligence of Kebuk/Ma-Son.

28. "When they Rise into this Spiritual Measure of Awareness, they will Raise Up a Nation that represents this **Order of I**nfinity - **S**ound - **L**ight - **A**nimating - **M**entalism, through their Natural Order of **I**ntelligence-Science-Law-**A**rchitecture-   and-**M**athematics   that   constructs **I**nfrastructure - of - **S**ymbolism - **L**abor - **A**ncestry - and - **M**orality.

29. "Solomon's Comprehension surrounded the basis of Hardcore Reality; and such was the Structure of Akh-Hulebuk's retained Lessons. For Akh-Hulebuk has Learning about Solomon's Knowledge of Hardcore Reality. And let this Be the Formula for the calculation of the next variable.

30. "Let it Be hereby Established for Solution of this Equational Variable: **Solution manifests, H**ardcore Reality in the **O**rder - of - Time-to bring Balance through the **E**volution - of **P**ure Infinite Energy; **The Gift of PEACE.**

31. "We shall Start Akh - Hulebuk on the Quest of Learning The Way, Discerning the Truth and being Servants of Light in Nuhfamuoh through the Guidance of the Gift of PEACE, that Solomon's perception of Hardcore Reality may manifest in degrees.

32. "Let Us Travel into Nuhfamuoh as an Infinite-Divine-Duality of the Male Gender and Masculine Principle, as the Gift of PEACE through the Seed of Solomon.

33. "As The Seed of Solomon to Akh-Hulebuk, We will BE the Gift of PEACE and Known as HOTEP; **Hotep the G**rand - **O**rder - **D**ivine of the Celestial expansions in the terrestrial plane; Hotep, the Spirit of Solomon manifested in flesh."

34. And the entire cast of Celestial hosts throughout Faluizzi prepared for The Gift of PEACE to Travel Within their measurements.

35. The Council of GODS All extended a part of their Spirit into The Hardcore Reality to manifest as Solomon's Seed.

36. And the Spirit of Solomon went through the Mansion's Sacred Halls, departing through the 90° Quadrant withholding the Gates of Fire as **H**ardcore Reality - in - the - **O**rder of - **T**ime to bring Balance through the -**E**volution of - **P**ure Infinite Energy.

$$\Longleftarrow \quad O - O - O - O - O \quad \Longrightarrow$$

CHAPTER IV
Hotep Raised Up and Taught the Natural Order of Masonry Through the Chambers of Atom and Evolution's Sacred Halls of Learning

1. In the Seasonal Cycle of Beginnings, a Ray of Light beamed into the Womb of Evolution, and a Sun was manifest.

2. Already informed of the Ordained coming of The Sun of Solomon's Seed, both Atom and Evolution addressed this Divine Light of God-Consciousness as Hotep.

3. Evolution looked into his eyes and said unto him: "Hotep-Kebuk - Sun of Nuhfamuoh, Ordained is your Coming into the Consciousness of The Present Moment to bring Akh-Hulebuk, the Hardcore Reality of The Light.

4. "For you have been sent down to us — The Parents of Solomon's manifestation in Nature and Akh-Hulebuk, to be Raised up through the Chambers of Natural Order. Your Education in our Sacred Halls of Learning Will Build Up your Character to Comprehend the Circumstances of degree standings of measurements for your assignment with Akh-Hulebuk Carpenter's Guild.

5. "You've come equipped with the 4 dimension's structures and

measurements of Balance; well Learned in the Hardcore Reality of manifesting **P**roductive – Education – that – **A**ctivates – **C**osmic - Energy. You've Traveled through the Mansion's Wheel, to Serve Nuhfamuoh with this Gift of PEACE.

6. "Comprehend the Circumstances; you are the working Light of a Spiritual Mathematical Equational Variable intended to bring the Hardcore Reality of The Light of Solomon to Akh-Hulebuk.

7. "Solomon's Light of Order cannot Be Structured in Balanced Measurements of **P**roductive – **E**ducation –Activating – **C**osmic - Energy, until you Travel our Chamber's Sacred Halls as a Student that builds into an Adept that Becomes a Master in the **I**ntelligence – of – **S**cience – **L**aw – **A**rchitecture – and - **M**athematics. You Were Sent to Us as Hotep-Kebuk The Sun of Solomon's Seed - Spiritual Light of The WORD and Will depart into The Natural Order of Natural, as Hoptep - The Master Mason - The Hardcore Reality of Light; the manifest Seed of Solomon constructing PEACE To Akh-Hulebuk."

8. As just a **P**ure **I**nfant **in Spirit**, Hotep looked into the eyes of Evolution and immediately bonded with her sense of vision.

9. Atom looked upon Solomon's Seed and seen that this God-Conscious Light would bring Order into Nuhfamuoh, through the Akh-Hulebuk Carpenter's Guild. He came to know his Wife; and Atom and Evolution gave Hotep transcendental garb.

10. Evolution held this **P**ure **I**nfant— now clothed in garb, and gave him Nurturing from her breast. She Raised the **P**ure **I**nfant to know every station he would need to know in dealing with establishing **I**ntelligence - of - **S**cience - **L**aw - **A**rchitecture - and - **M**athematics in Nature's Order.

11.   Atom took the **Pure Infant** through 3 different stages of **Gaining - Obtaining** - Development consisting of various degrees and measurements of Building the **Generating** – **Operating** - **Distributing Balance** of Comprehending the Circumstances of establishing **the Infrastructures** – **S**ymbolism – of - Labor's – **A**ncestry – and - **M**orality **of Solomon's perception of Hardcore Reality**. Evolution Nourished him with Vision and Formula.

12.   And Hotep went through most of The Sacred Halls, developing GOD sense and Purpose. Atom taught him to use every Spiritual Tool required to Build Balance in Nuhfamuoh. He'd Mastered every degree and measurement to manufacture **I**nfrastructures - of - **S**ymbolism with the - **L**abors - of - **A**ncestral - **M**orality into Nuhfamuoh and Nature's Rule.

13.   When Hotep Thought his Learning was complete, he was asked to take a walk with Evolution into A Plane of Sight. And he Walked with her as she said unto him: "Hotep-Kebuk, you've been promoted through the Sacred Halls and now have the mechanical God-Consciousness to construct Homeostasis.

14.   "Atom and I have Served you according to the Divine Plan of the Council of GODS. Through the Mansions of Fire, you have seen the Face of The Great I AM illuminate Hardcore Reality with Its indescribable Beauty.

15.   "Hence, in Faluizzi, you are the one who Sees through the Eyes of The Great I AM, and Will enter Nuhfamuoh as The Seed of Solomon and Master Mason."

16.   And Hotep said unto her: "Through the first Mansion of Fire's Gate did I acquire the Spiritual Education of ALLAH - The Great I AM.

37

I Mastered the Sacred Halls of Learning in The Mansions of Fire, Mansions of Land, Mansions of Air and Mansions of Water through the **Order of** Infinity - **S**ound - **L**ight - **A**nimation - and - **M**entalism.

17.   "My assignment is to Teach Akh-Hulebuk the Harmonies of Life, and how to construct Spiritual Hardcore Reality into manifest with Purpose, that the Natural Order may develop **I**nfrastructure – Symbolism – Labor – Ancestry – and - **M**orality **as Servants.**

18.   "And it is because of Atom's and Evolution's Chambers of Natural Order that I See the Way to establish the Truth about Solomon's perception of Hardcore Reality in The Light; but it is because of ALLAH The Great I AM; Father and Ruler of The Universe, that I will establish the **I**nfrastructures-and-**S**ymbolisms- with-**L**abors – in – **A**ncestral - **M**orality **of Solomon's vision in Light of the WORD,** to construct Balance in Nuhfamuoh and Solve the variable of the Council of GODS.

19.   "Through the Chambers with The Sacred Halls of Learning the Balance of Spiritual Homeostasis, I can and will Teach Akh-Hulebuk to Build Natural Homeostasis in every degree and dimensional measurement of Nuhfamuoh.

20.   "So it shall BE declared: **I**nfinite **S**ight Will bring **I**ntelligent **S**olution **through H**ardcore Reality - in the - **O**rder - of - **T**ime - to bring Balance through the - **E**volution - of - **P**ure Infinite Energy."

21.   Evolution was pleased with Hotep's reply. She grabbed his hand as they continued their Journey. And She said unto him: "Through me, all Pure Infinite Energy must have Balance in Calculations and measurements of time.

22.   "The things that you will see Hotep—Kebuk amongst Man in

calculated spans of measured time, Will change One from the other. Solomon's perception of Hardcore Reality brought into manifest Natural Order by You, Will not change.

23. "Measuring the Various degrees on the Pole Will Only give the appearance that Hardcore Reality has changed. It has not. What you must Teach Akh-Hulebuk about this appearance, is how Past Activity can be reviewed in Consciousness to make preparation for Future activity in the Present Moment. For these are both sides of the Pole in Solomon's Vision.

24. "No, it is not Hardcore Reality of Solomon's Vision in such an analysis that changes, but rather the degree measurements in dimensional ranges of standings through Solomon's perception of Hardcore Reality changes.

25. "There's a standing called 'Under'-standing, where Consciousness dimensionally travels into degree measurements of Depth, intaking the profoundness of All Intellectualism.

26. "There's a standing called 'Over'-standing, where Consciousness dimensionally Travels into degree measurements of Height, being Elevated by Intellectual Order.

27. "As you were Taught in the Sacred Halls, your Plumbline is the Tool utilized in Conscious matters of 'Under' and 'Over' standings, as they are dimensionally measured in degrees of Depth and Height.

28. "There's a standing called 'Inner'-standing, where Consciousness dimensionally Travels from the Balance on The Pole into degree measurements of Width, widening the peripheral vision of Consciousness for involuntary Intelligence.

29. "There's a standing called 'Outer'-standing, where Consciousness dimensionally Travels from the Balance on The Pole into degree measurements of Length, extending the Central stability of Intelligence from Negative to Positive Fields.

30. "As you were Taught in the Sacred Halls, your Plane is the tool utilized in Conscious matters of 'Inner and 'Outer' standings as they are dimensionally measured in degrees of Length and Width.

31. "As we Journey down the Plane of Sight, Lo, Hotep-Kebuk, the standings that Akh-Hulebuk must learn to Discern, to Service Nuhfamuoh With Order, are incorporated into The Tools you must Teach.

32. "2 of the Standings are Over and Under and for perpendicular Sight that the Plumb Line is used to construct Comprehension and two of the standings are Inner and Outer and for level Sight that the Plane is used for construction of Comprehension.

33. "Akh-Hulebuk must BE Taught by you, how to receive perpendicular vision in standings on the Atlas, and rotate All Comprehension of level vision in standings around the Axis.

34. "Say of I Evolution in the Right Time, that I showed you as well as Nourished you from the suck of my Breast, these Supreme Formulas of Natural Solution."

35. Hotep knew of the Formula he was fed from her Breast, but didn't recall of any sight of it. And he said unto the Great Evolution: "Oh Mother of Natural Metamorphosis, I Comprehend well the use of the Tools constructing perpendicular and level Standings and Will Teach Akh-Hulebuk the Mathematical application of Formula for Service in

Nuhfamuoh with this Masonry. I **have in fact been Nourished with the Formulas of Natural Solution that gives the** Intellectual – Scientific – Lawful – Architectural - Mathematical **perceptual basis of Solomon's vision of constructing Homeostasis**. But Evolution-Mother of Natural Metamorphosis, I have no factual sight of Its designer."

36.   And Evolution said unto him: "Hotep-Kebuk, when you looked me in my Eyes, unveiled to you was The Vision of the Formula. You have been given Solomon's Sense of Vision as the Equational Solution in Spiritual Variable. Where you are Traveling, none other has had the Vision of the Formula.

37.   "Through Me, Hotep, you have seen the Formula of Natural Solution. Your Journey through this Plane of Sight is one on the Spiritual Axis, where you Oh Kebuk, are granted the ability to See the Mathematical Equations, and Solve their complexities. Through Solomon's Sense of Vision, You See and You Solve."

38.   They stopped at the Height of a Mountain among surrounding Hills where they looked out across a Sea of Electrical Sands. And there was a Bush on the Mountain that appeared to be on Fire, but did not burn.

39.   And Evolution said unto Hotep: "This is the Meeting Place that you have been Blessed to see. Look at the Firey Sands on the ground. Do you See the number of Sands?"

40.   Hotep answered Evolution: "The Sands appear to be on Fire; they are burning with the Light of God-Consciousness, but do not burn with any flames that turns things to ash.

41. "It is the Pure Infinite Energy that Rises through those Sands as Fire, and can only be determined in number through me.

42. "I See the Energy of Fire Within the Sands that makes them visible in hundreds of billions. And the determined number can only be calculated as **Pure Infinite Energy of GOD-Consciousness**." It was then that Hotep began comprehending seeing the Formula of Natural Solution.

43. Evolution walked through the Fire of the Burning Bush and brought Hotep with her, and he seen the Portal Doorway into Faluizzi and beyond. At the Doorway, he saw an inscription on the top post, along with a key.

44. **The inscription read:**

$$\textbf{Keahbu-Dūhāh•-Nuhlē•/•} \quad \vdash - \cdot \triangle - \, \text{}\backslash \cdot \, \Upsilon \, ;$$

and it meant, MAN, Know Thyself. It was the only Way that The Master's Key was reachable, that opened the Portal Doors into Faluizzi and beyond.

45. And Evolution said unto him: "Hotep-Kebuk, you must Teach Akh-Hulebuk all that you See, and Solve the Equational Solution's Variable. Behold the Portal Doors and **the inscription that is the Pass WORD,** granting access to the Master's Key to unlock the Doors for entry.

46. "Look beyond Faluizzi and gaze upon the **Youniversal/Universal Ladder**. See the expansions of **M**entalism – **A**nimating - **N**avigation, See the Celestial hosts and Comprehend their visibility in the hundreds of billions as they are illuminated by the unburning Fires of Pure Infinite

Energy of God-Consciousness." Hotep obeyed Evolution; and they stepped out of the Fire of the Burning Bush that didn't burn, and began walking down the Mountain.

47.   Hotep realized that his Walk With Evolution - The Mother of Natural Metamorphosis, was more than just a stroll through the Plane of Sight; it was an important class and Lesson being Taught by her to him.

48.   And they both stood at the Surface of the Mountain at the beginning of the Firey, Electrically Charged Sands. The unburning Fire of the Sands had a Geometric Tide that made things appear to Hotep's Sight. There Was an **Arithmetical** setting, an **Algebraic** Fall spawning from a **Geometric** Rise of Fire through; within the Sands.

49.   Hotep seen 24 Elders sitting on 24 Thrones surrounding The Mountain with the Burning Bush that didn't burn. They were 12 on each side of the Mountain.

And there were 3 Tracts withholding a 4 walled Governmental Palace. It All appeared Geometrically with a Great Rise, disappeared Algebraically with a misty Fall, and sat for Sight Arithmetically as Fire coming out of The Sands that Surrounded One Divine Throne on The Mountain.

50.   And Evolution said unto him: "You must walk these Firey Sands and learn to Comprehend what you See in every degree measurement.

51.   "In this Circle of 7, learn to See the Spiritual Significance of your main tools for Building this Governmental Palace, and All that you See sit, rise and fall through the Firey Sands, Arithmetically, Geometrically and Algebraically.

52.   **"Hotep-Kebuk, you are the Pure Infinite Energy of God-**

Consciousness - the Spiritual Fire within the Sands. The totality of the things that you see coming out of the Sands of Fire are encompassed by you.

53. "To Build the **I**nfrastructures – **S**ymbolism – of – **L**abors – in - Ancestral-**M**orality **of Solomon's perception of Hardcore Reality, you must go down into Nuhfamuoh, Comprehending Kebuk, that you are the Spiritual meaning Within the Natural Compass.**

54. "As I AM with you now Hotep-Kebuk, I Will always Be With you. When you Teach the mechanics of Building all that you encompass, you will Teach about me as I AM the Formula Source of Solution that raises Consciousness in Stages of exact degree measurements.

55. "The mechanics of the things you see Geometrically standing through the Fiery Sands and the basis of All Standings in Height, Depth, Width, and Length are measured by me, The Square.

56. "To Build the Infrastructures-Symbolism-of-Labors-in-Ancestral-Morality of Solomon's perception of Hardcore Reality, you must go down into Nuhfamuoh, Comprehending Kebuk, that I AM the Spiritual meaning of the Intelligent Solution Within the **Natural Square**.

57. "The Compass and the Square are symbolic of the Circle and the 7 in every degree measurement. You are the Infinite Sight of Solomon that will draw out Hardcore Reality in Nuhfamuoh through the Intelligent-Science-of-Law-Architecture- and-Mathematics of the Natural Compass; I AM the Intelligent Solution of Solomon's vision as it rises in degree stages of God-Consciousness through the Natural Square. You See, I Solve; put them together and You See -You Solve.

58. "Just as the Celestial Mansions are in 4 teams of 3 that manifests

12, but encompasses the Wheel that Houses the symbol of Perfection in 7 Above, so it is Below, only through the Building up of Nuhfamuoh.

59. "Nothing Hotep-Kebuk, can stand without being raised up in degree by me. In All Measures of standings, the God-Consciousness of All Mentalisms must stand on the Square to be Raised Up.

60. "Nothing will Evolve through me Without being brought into the Full Circle of Order—within which the Square resides, by you. See, and then Solve this Vision by Teaching the Akh-Hulebuk Carpenter's Guild, Hardcore Reality.

61. "To be a part of Building up Nuhfamuoh, All must Stand on The Square within the Circle in 720°, to evoke the Mystical Presence of their Ancestors and their God-Consciousness. I AM the Spiritual quality Within the Square. You are the Hardcore Reality within the Compass/Circle."

62. They began walking through the Fiery Sands together. Hotep seen the sounds of the Electrical Fires as they rose from the Sands. As they walked, the Domain of Nuhfamuoh Geometrically, Algebraically and Arithmetically Revealed itself to him through Evolution's eyes.

63. And they made it all the way across the entire expansion into a dwelling place where caves and rocky grounds resided. The Mountain from which they descended seemed to fit in his hand.

64. And he said unto her: "I Hotep-Kebuk, have Traveled the Course across the Fiery, Electrically Charged Sands and have seen the Blue Print to the Raising Up of Nuhfamuoh through your Eyes.

65. "**I AM, the Pure Infinite Energy of God - Consciousness** within

the Circle which is Perfected in the 7 I Symbolically Encompass; and you are the measurements of my development which is Square; you are the means of Insight; I AM, the means of Infinite Sight that will bring Intelligent Solution.

66. "Hence, we together, construct Intelligence, Measurements of developmental Science, the basis of All-Law and All Architectural Mathematical Equational Substance that Rises.

67. "Oh Evolution - Mother of Natural Metamorphosis, I will Teach of you in the Right Time, saying you are the one who fed, as well as showed me the Formula of Natural Solution. And I Will Say to All, that her Nurturing Name is ISIS; which means I See I Solve.

68. "All will Know that ISIS walked me across the Electrically Charged Fiery Sands, Up and down the Mountain with the Burning Bush that does not Burn, into the Fire, through the Fire and into complete Comprehension of Hardcore Reality in the Order of Time to bring Balance through the Evolution of Pure Infinite Energy With Sound Visual of Intelligence – Science – Law – Architecture – and – Mathematics, constructed in Signs of Compass and Square that represents the Universal Circled 7.

69. "I Will Teach Akh-Hulebuk as you have Taught me, that Infinite Sight will bring Intelligent Solution, **only when your veil is removed** and you're allowed to Nurture and Show them the Portal Doors that has inscribed on its post above:

Keahbu-Dūhāh-Nuhlē/

70. "I Will Be your glowing example, Mother of Natural Metamorphosis, as you Be my measuring Guide - Orchestrating - Degree

- Direction - in - **E**volutionary - **S**upreme - **S**olutions."

71.   Evolution smiled and hugged Hotep. She knew that by him naming her ISIS, he did in fact Comprehend her Teachings.

72.   She continued Teaching him about the Tools, their use in Nuhfamuoh, and walking him through the Plane of Sight, working with him in calculated Time, Raising him up into a Master of Time.

73.   And Every Law, Architectural, Mathematical Angle was Mastered by Hotep, for the Building up of Nuhfamuoh.

74.   In the appointed Time, Hotep was promoted from the Master's degree in the Sacred Halls Plane of Sight and given the Master's Key to the Portal Doors.

75.   And Hotep left Evolution to become structured into The Rhythmic Order of Time.

$$\Longleftarrow \quad O - O - O - O - O \quad \Longrightarrow$$

CHAPTER V
Hotep Enters Nuhfamuoh and Raised by a Builder of Shelters

1. In Nuhfamuoh, the Natural Man generationally advanced into traditional motions. Utilizing the Skills Taught to them by their Ancient Ancestors, Solomon's Order reigned Supreme.

2. Akh-Hulebuk were the Masters who were taught by Solomon, the Source of their Ancient Ancestry. Utilizing the Building techniques Solomon Taught as being the mechanical craft of the 7 Sources of Natural establishment, Akh-Hulebuk constructed Tools, Shelters and Survival Skills.

3. All who learned the craft of laboring with the Natural Tools, were important to Nuhfamuoh's health. All prestigious Masters of the Carpenter's Craft, were direct descendents of Solomon.

4. Solomon's descendents kept the Teaching alive, of one to come from the Divine Seed, to Teach a Divine Service with the Workings of the Tools beyond their current Comprehension, that will Build Nuhfamuoh up into The Supreme Order as Kebuk - Sun of the Mother/Mason.

5. And there was a young Master of the Akh - Hulebuk Carpenter's Guild highly skilled in Building Shelters, and studious Teacher to newcomers about the Tools and their use and meanings. The name of this young Master was Baduh•.

6.   Descended from the Seed of Solomon's Wealth, from the Ancient lineage of 7 Sources, was a **G**uide – **O**rchestrating – **D**egree – **D**irection – in – **E**volutionary – **S**upreme - **S**olutions of Nuhfamuoh's establishment named Mahle: And Mahle was married to Baduh during that era of Time.

7.   A unique force in Union and significant portion of Akh-Hulebuk Carpenters Guild, both Mahle and Baduh were admirable in their duties and uplifting affairs.

8.   Baduh came to know his Wife, and she conceived his seed. In early stages of carrying the seed, Mahle noticed that something was different about her process than what she'd seen with others in their process.

9.   Mahle experienced her child communicating with her in her periods of rest, explaining the meanings to things she'd never Thought of.

10. And it came to pass in the 9th stage of Mahle's carrying process that in her rest, her child came to her. They were in a place that seemed like Nuhfamuoh, but was far more advanced than what Mahle knew.

11. And she said unto the child: "My child, my child, why do you come to me in this form? I AM confused and unsure of the meaning of your arrivals."

12. The child walked up to his Mother and grabbed her hand. He pointed out into the expansions of the land and he said unto her: "Mahle, my Mother, there are no Strange happenings. You are the Mother of this Child who will Raise up Nuhfamuoh in this degree construction.

13. **"I come to you as The Light of The WORD; it is in this form, that Hardcore Reality manifests in Nuhfamuoh as P**ure Infinite

50

Energy of God - Consciousness. Forms outside of this form change and pass away.

14.   "Do not fear Hardcore Reality! For that which seems to be Real in Nuhfamuoh outside of God-Consciousness is not, such things change through Authoritative measurements of Time. Perception of the Light of the WORD measures in degrees through Solomon's Vision; the Natural experience thereof is not Real.

15.   "Lo, that which seems to be unreal in Nuhfamuoh is the Actuality of Hardcore Reality. The Light of The WORD constructs the Pure Infinite Energy of God- Consciousness, that projects Hardcore Reality. Mahle, my Mother, I AM Hardcore Reality. I AM, Real.

16.   "Your Natural form under the Authoritative measurement of Time is at rest, while your Reality is not. The Natural Man's existence is mere vibrational sound that begins and ends. Spirit MAN Masters the measurement Time extends and Raises up to the Reality of I AM. Your Reality is Hardcore Reality which surpasses Time's Calculations, of Vibrational Sounds in Motion's appearing still.

17.   "Time has no Authority over Light. In Nuhfamuoh, the Spirit MAN at large is at rest as your natural form in the measurement of Time is right now. The problem is the unknowing fact of Spiritual Unawareness being the prevalent rest factor while the Natural man in form is up and functioning.

18.   "There's no Comprehension of Solomon's Perception which is why Solomon spoke of one to come from the seed of Reality, to Teach a Divine Service that Will manifest Supreme Order in Nuhfamuoh. You, Mahle, are the Evolutionary Matriarch. I AM, Hotep-Kebuk, the Sun of you - the Goddess Mother."

19.   Mahle listened to Hotep. The Revelation was spoken to her, of the coming of Supreme Order. Hotep explained to his Mother the contractions and expansions of Holy Breath. The scene changed into an advanced Setting of Nuhfamuoh as they took a calculated walk through unburning Fire.

20.   The unburning Fire became clear, still waters upon which Hotep stood. It was a great body of water that Hotep stepped out on and did not sink into. Mahle found herself in a ship looking at him. He reached out his hand and said unto her: "Mahle, my Mother, exit the ship and come to me. For within the Waters, there's the unburning Fire of Hardcore Reality."

21.   Mahle looked into the waters and became reluctant. And she said unto him: "My child, there's no solid ground upon which I could stand that I may take any steps towards your position. If I enter the Fire Water, I will drown."

22.   Hotep looked into, and then across the expansion of the great body of water. He stared into his Mother's eyes and said unto her: "Mahle, my Mother, there are 4 standings measured in degrees of God— Consciousness and 3 that are relevant in these Circumstances.

23.   "There's Over-standing, where MAN'S perception must reach into the Heights for Comprehension. There's Under-standing, where the preception of MAN must reach into the Depths for Comprehension, there's Inner-standing, where the perception of MAN must reach into the Width of situations for comprehension and there's Outer-standing, Where the perception of MAN must reach at Length into situations for Comprehension.

24.   "Utilize your 'standings' to Comprehend that the Heat of the Light

of the WORD is a Fire that makes solid grounds, into liquid grounds, into gaseous grounds.

25. "Within transcendental garb, you Mahle, my Mother are beyond Authoritative measurements of Time, in the expansions of the Light of The WORD. Through the contractions and expansions of Holy Breath, you have entered the Realm of Over-standing. All things are possible according to your standings in Hardcore Reality.

26. "Exit the Ship Mother Goddess and come to me. There's no drowning in Hardcore Reality."

27. Mahle obeyed and stepped out onto the waters. She walked the Waters towards Hotep, noticing her perception reflecting him moving towards her, rather than her towards him.

28. She looked into the waters and seen an unburning Fire on a Mountain in Nuhfamuoh, surrounded by 12 Thrones on its left Side and 12 Thrones on its right. Nuhfamuoh was being built up by Solomon's descendants. She grabbed Hotep's hand in awe.

29. And he said unto her: "Behold, as you stand on the Spiritual Atlas and gaze into Nuhfamuoh's Order. You are now in the Heights, Overstanding the Depths of Reality that is Hardcore.

30. "The Ship that sits on the Atlas is your duty to Build in Nuhfamuoh. It is the Mothership that sails Solomon's Vision across the celestial Waters and Into the grounds where you see 24 Elders Surrounding the Throne on the Mountain where the Unburning Fire of the Bush resides.

31. "Within the Mothership is the Blue Print to Mother's Building the

Universal Temple of Solomon. This is a Blue Print drawn up by ISIS the Supreme Goddess and Mother of Natural Metamorphosis explaining the Building up of Solomon's Temple Without any Tools. Take of the Blue Print and eat it whole."

32.   Obedient to Hotep's command, Mahle walked back into the Ship, took of the Blue Print, and ate it whole. And she looked out across the waters, seeing Solomon sit on a Throne on the 4th stair of a Universal Ladder. Hotep was gone. Solomon looked into the Eyes of Mahle, making her Short of Breath.

33.   And Solomon said unto her: "Mahle - child of my Wealth, the most valuable jewel from my Treasure Chest is God Degree. I AM the Soul of MAN. The Soul is The Consciousness of the Present Moment, capable of Comprehending the Circumstances of Hardcore Reality.

34.   "MAN is the **M**entalism – **A**nimating - the - **N**avigation of **The** Intelligence of **A**ll – **M**otion; The I AM of the Great I AM. The Spirit is the ALL'S WORD, the Soul is the Light.

35.   "The Soul—being the Light of the Spirit MAN, has the ability to perceive every frequency of Vibration the WORD speaks. Perception is Thinking and retaining degree Comprehension of Hardcore Reality.

36.   "Another valuable jewel, oh daughter of the Light, is Beauty. Beauty is the unfrozen Motion of Perception that constructs every standing to measure Consciousness of the Present Moment in Balance with God Order.

37.   "There is no stand still in Beauty. **The M**entalism of **A**nimate **N**avigational **Power in God - Consciousness is a Crown of Gold**. This Crown is worn by the Light of the WORD, and manifests through your

SUN - Hotep-Kebuk.

38. "There are various jewels of Wealth from which you descended. There's Patience, there's Faith, there's Compassion, there's Sincerity, there's Seriousness, there's Discipline and Motivation, all making Solomon shine in Beauty and God-degree.

39. "Hotep is the Light of the WORD, wearing Solomon's Jewels and is the Mason that will Proclaim I AM upon manifestation in the Natural Plane.

40. "Daughter of Light, give Birth to the Gaining-Obtaining-Development of Nuhfamuoh. This is The Cultivation of I AM; and you shall call his name Hotep- Kebuk."

41. Mahle was awestruck. She stood upon the Waters of Fire, looking up at Solomon, as Solomon sat in the Throne on the 4th Stair of the Universal Ladder.

42. She tried going to him and fell into the Firey Waters, sinking fast. Just as she was about to panic, she woke from her rest, jumping from the intensity of her dream. She realized that she was in her bed, in her shelter, perspiring profusely.

43. And Mahle looked around the room in wonder. She rubbed her stomach and said aloud: "Hotep-Kebuk, from the Wisdom, Strength and Beauty of Solomon's vision will you don the crown of Honor in Nuhfamuoh."

44. Baduh entered the room to find Mahle awake. And she said unto him: "Baduh, the Time is near for our child to enter this world. For I have seen yet again, that it is a male child who will be the one spoken of

to come and Build up Nuhfamuoh from the Seed of Solomon.

45. "I've seen Solomon sit on the Throne beyond our scope, explaining to me the Cultivation of I AM as the Light of the WORD wearing Solomon's Jewels. The child to come through me shall BE called Hotep-Kebuk.

46. "Hotep-Kebuk will enter Nubfamuoh when Fire erupts from the most distant Mountain North of this Land, where there are sands and a Great Body of Water."

47. Baduh said to his Wife: "Solomon spoke of a decision maker, Educator, leader and Servant to come and define degrees of Intelligence-Science-Law- Architecture-and-Mathematics with the perceptual awareness of God-Consciousness.

48. "The Akh-Hulebuk Carpenters Guild are the reigning heirs to sit in Solomon's Throne. None of their wives say the things that you say. Such things can get us ridiculed and challenged.

49. "There's no way that you can Be the Mother of Solomon's Seed. Mahle, we've been into every Hill and valley North of this land. There has been none but I Baduh, Skilled enough or capable of climbing that Mountain of which you speak, much less build anything around it."

50. Mahle grabbed Baduh and made him sit down. She rubbed his face and said to him: "As sure as the circular sphere of Fire residing in the sky illuminates over the Mountain and Lights up Nuhfamuoh, Solomon's Seed will manifest from my Womb.

51. "You Baduh, are the chosen leadership in the Akh-Hulebuk Carpenters Guild, blessed to say of the child that will come, that you are

the Parent responsible for Raising him Up.

52.   "Solomon's Seed is your seed. None can say what I say unto you because none have seen Solomon and Solomon's Seed as have I.

53.   "The child has revealed to me to say to you that, in the Time of his arrival, the distant Mountain North that only you could climb, will erupt with Fire. And in that moment, he will come through that Fire and enter this World through me. You shall name him in that Time, Hotep-Kebuk."

54.   Baduh agreed reluctantly and affectionately comforted Mahle.

55.   And it came to pass in the 5th Hour after Mahle's dream, that she went into labor. Things in Nuhfamuoh changed into unusual events.

56.   As Mahle's water broke, the waters around the distant Mountain crashed violently, as the Fire within it stirred.

57.   While in the delivery process, the Akh-Hulebuk Carpenter's Guild stood in distant wonder, analyzing the rumbling that emerged from the Mountain.

58.   And a Ball of Fire shot from out of the sky and into the great body of water surrounding the distant Mountain. The Mountain erupted with liquid Fire soon after, shooting High in the sky.

59.   A Sudden Darkness surrounded Nuhfamuoh for a time, as liquid Fire shot from the Mountain and filled the great body of Water, making it glow with Light. In that moment, Mahle gave birth to her child.

60.   The skies cleared and Light was back manifest in the Sky, as the Mountain stopped erupting. The Akh-Hulebuk Carpenters Guild were

amazed by the Great signs, all agreeing amongst the elite of one another, that the Great Signs were the coming of Solomon's Seed.

61.   The Child did not weep upon delivery as had done children before it. After the Child's umbilical cord was cut, it was laid into Mahle's arms.

62.   Baduh was amazed by the Signs, and humbled by their aligning into Mahle's dreams. He immediately fixed his Mentalism to hold the Child in reverence as it was the manifest Gift of PEACE through Solomon's Seed.

63.   He was called into the Shelter and away from the Akh-Hulebuk Carpenters, to witness the manifestation of the Seed of Solomon. Mahle said unto him: "It is a male child as I have told you Baduh, who came through the Fire of the Sky, erupting the Fire through the distant Mountain."

64.   Baduh looked upon the child and wept in utter joy. He grabbed the child and held him up to the sky.

65.   And Baduh declared aloud: "Oh Maker and Molder of Solomon; Father of All Things; High Power of the Fires in the distant Mountain; I name the Gift of PEACE as You have confirmed his name to be through his Mother.

66.   "I deliver unto you Oh Maker and Molder of Solomon, Hotep-Kebuk."

67.   Baduh handed Mahle the child in utter amazement. Mahle spoke to the child and said to him: "Hotep, I AM Mahle, your Mother. The things you have shown me has prepared me to assist you in your works.

68.   "You've dropped your Anchor in Nuhfamuoh as you've exited the

Mother Ship. I submit to you right now as my Master, Willing to Serve according to your wishes. As the speaking of your coming was the hope of Akh-Hulebuk, we are prepared to Raise you up that we may Be Raised Up."

69.   Baduh kneeled down on his knees and raised both hands into the sky with joy. And he said aloud: "Oh Father of All Things, we recognize You in Hotep- Kebuk. Let Solomon's Seed Continue Solomon's deed that Order may manifest from Chaos."

70.   Hotep stared at his Natural Mother and Father in Silence. When the excitement of the moment finally decreased, he wept as would any child.

71.   And both Mahle and Baduh Raised Up Hotep as the Natural Parents of Solomon's Seed, teaching him the Intelligence-Science-Law-Architecture-and-Mathematics of Solomon's vision for the Natural Order.

72.   The Akh-Hulebuk Carpenters Guild treated Hotep like a jewel, knowing that a Time would come when he would unfold a Higher Standard than what they knew.

73.   Hotep grew gracefully, vibrant, full of Natural information and was very inquisitive. He became the youngest member of the Akh-Hulebuk Carpenters Guild; and he became addicted to the Order of Solomon's Teachings.

⇐ O — O — O — O — O ⇒

CHAPTER VI
Hotep Teaches Buduh about the Tools and His Mother and Father The Purpose of Existence

1.   The Circle of Life spun and Hotep was 7 years into existence. Mahle raised him to Comprehend the values and morals of their culture, while Baduh taught him the means of survival.

2. Baduh made sure that Hotep Comprehended the Builder's Craft while still young. He worked with Hotep as he would any other Student, teaching Akh-Hulebuk's Blue Prints, from Solomon.

3. And he took Hotep into the shed where he kept his Tools, to rehearse with him their use and purpose. Baduh said unto him: "I'm going to see to it that you become a Master Mason as I AM, in the Akh-Hulebuk Carpenters Guild. Building shelters will be your profession in Nuhfamuoh."

4.   After they were done rehearsing the lessons of the day, Hotep looked upon the Tools as they were laid out on the ground. And he said unto Baduh: "Father, every lesson you teach your Students in the Carpenters Guild should beget a lesson of Hardcore Reality.

5. "These tools are for building shelter from the transitional conditions of Seasonal Motions. You teach this craft well. Know that MAN is more

than the laborer with these Tools. You must learn to teach that Solomon's Blue Print teaches of MAN also being the Spiritual designer of them.

6. "You've taught about Solomon and the Ancient Ancestor's crafts that designed the Tools here in Nuhfamuoh. You've taught nothing of the Ancient Ancestors and Solomon's Educational platform.

7. "The Ancient Ancestry of the Akh-Hulebuk Carpenters Guild were taught by Solomon, who Traveled the course of schooling in the Sacred Halls of Learning as did I, to enter Nuhfamuoh, to Teach the Intelligence-Science-Law-Architecture and-Math of Ark Building.

8. "The Ancestors of Solomon's era could not grasp the totality of the Carpenters Guild, leaving them to only learn the external fundamentals of Shelter Building.

9. "Generations passed through times Authoritative Measurements without any to Teach the Akh-Hulebuk Carpenters the totality of Solomons vision of Building Shelters. For it is more than just erecting external exoteric structures. The vision of Solomon was also for Akh-Hulebuk Carpenters to learn the Building of Structures from an internal, esoteric Hardcore Reality.

10. "**From the Gaining - Obtaining - Developing knowledge of both Building abilities, Akh-Hulebuk would Be able to construct the Ark of Hardcore Reality as a Safe haven for Nuhfamuoh's Order**.

11. "Solomon meant for these Tools to Be more than just Builders of exoteric, external structure. **To learn the Blue Print of Solomon's Masonary, Akh-Hulebuk must Be Taught that these Tools are Builders and Molders of 1. Character, 2. Comprehension of**

Hardcore Realism, and 3. All Circumstances thereof.

12. **"In an era and time measurement outside of this Present Moment, Man of Natural Order Will be lost and fully incapable of reading Solomon's Blue Prints. You must Learn to construct the Ark of Hardcore Reality as visioned by Solomon, that the people of that time may find refuge in THE GREAT GOD of The Universe through the Service of Akh-Hulebuk.**

13. "Lo, Nuhfamuoh cannot properly stand in Balance until the Carpenters Guild learns the Purpose, meaning and basis of Order. **I AM Hotep-Kebuk, the L**awful - **A**rchitectural - **M**athematical – **B**asis, and have come to Nuhfamuoh to show you the construction of such Order with these Tools in 3 stages, with 4 dimensional degree measurements.

14. "And the First Stage of Building to Be brought into manifest here in Nuhfamuoh through Akh-Hulebuk is Character. Every Tool here represents a device to construct quality Temperament, habit, complexion, and reflection aligning with Spiritual Balance.

15. "Through All Standings, Akh-Hulebuk must be Raised up to be a living Perpendicular on the Atlas of Hardcore Reality. The Height of Character should expand beyond the ideal of survival, into Sacrificial Service.

16. The Depth of Character should Travel deep into the Intellectualism of Solomon's perception of Hardcore Reality, that the Akh-Hulebuk Carpenters Guild may live according to their intended Purpose of Raising Up Nuhfamuoh into Order, and Building the Ark that will Be the refuge for The People.

17. "The Second Stage of Building to Be brought into manifest here in

Nuhfamuoh, through Akh-Hulebuk is Comprehension of Hardcore Reality. When Akh-Hulebuk Comprehends the internal esoteric meanings of the Tools, All standings will align with the never ending Reality that is Hardcore.

18. "The Carpenters Guild could then step out into the unlimited grounds and learn from Solomon, the many luxuries and qualities molded into jewels within the Treasure Chest by his Throne. Such a Comprehension, will align Akh-Hulebuk and Nuhfamuoh into One function, as the Natural Mother will Birth this Comprehension of Hardcore Reality into the Manifest of the Present Moment, and Nourish it from the Suck of her Breast.

19. "Temperament of Akh-Hulebuk defines Character; Character of the Natural Man varies in complexions that make specific instinctive habits. When this is Comprehended in the use of these Tools then the Carpenters Guild and Nuhfamuoh will reign Supreme.

20. "The Third Stage of Building to Be brought into manifest here in Nuhfamuoh through Akh-Hulebuk is the establishment of Circumstances that Hardcore Reality exhibits. Akh-Hulebuk must Comprehend, that Hardcore Reality speaks in Infinite - Sounds - and - Lights - Animating - Mentalism. This is the Way into hearing Solomon's voice when he speaks.

21. "Sounds are the Vibrations Traveling throughout Infinity Comprehended by those that can see and hear, as Light. Every degree measurement dimensionally exhibits a range Frequency of Light that will Translate such an establishment of Circumstances Mentally.

22. "These Tools are The Gift of/from Solomon, handed down to the Ancient Ancestors, and manufactured to construct in Akh-Hulebuk,

Quality Character to Comprehend Hardcore Reality, that the establishment of Circumstances may give to us in Nuhfamuoh, the Building vision of Cosmic Nationals that will Rule the Natural. This is the Purpose, meaning and basis.

23. "The dimensional degree measurements are unlimited throughout the Youniverse. The Dark Waters of the Cosmic Mother's Womb gives Akh-Hulebuk the leverage to stand on the Atlas and Build up Nuhfamuoh on the Axis.

24. "The Father of the Youniverse speaks through the Hardcore Reality of every degree measurement. The Father of the Youniverse is ALLAH, the Great Infallible Architect of Mentalism, Designer of Lights Vibrational Ranges of Frequency.

25. "Our Ancient Ancestry are the direct descendants of the 7 Sources, and Youniverse of Mentalism. Atom and Evolution Became the Parents of All that is Natural. During his reign in the Natural, Solomon Ruled with the Intelligent Science of Law Architecture and Mathematics of the Council of GODS and gave to Nuhfamuoh the Akh-Hulebuk Carpenters.

26. "In this era, Akh-Hulebuk is the Spiritual Mentalism Animating Navigation amalgamated into a station called the Natural Molecular-Autonomical-Nucleus. Our Spirit of Mentalism in this Natural station of MAN is measured by The Square and drawn out in completion by the Compass.

27. "When Building Character, you must Teach that it has a Double Door. One Side of the Door gives entry into the Heights of the Natural Man's abilities, and the other side gives entry into the Depths of the Natural Man's abilities.

28.   "Juxtapositioned from the Balance of these Double Doors, there are Roads Directioning the Length and Width of the Natural Man's Mental capacity, where Character can be classified Temperamentally in Negative and Positive Fields of Frequency.

29.   "All of these compositional components of Character, are measured by the Square, as we in Balance of this Tool and its layers of meanings and Teachings, take all translated Sound of measurement to every distance diametrically representing the Width of Length in Height and Depth.

30.   "In All standings in dimensional measurements, the Spirit MAN - as the symbolic encompassing structure in Faluizzi, must stand on the Square, as Natural transitions of Gaining-Obtaining-Developing Power occur in the Balance of the Authoritative measurement of Time.

31.   "As the Compass, the Spirit MAN completes the Journey Traveled in the Natural as it is circumscribed by the celestial Forces of Government. And we as Spirit MAN in Faluizzi are the descendants of the Sources of Equational Solutions, and vested with the Generating-Operating-Distributing Power, to Build upon these Primordial Principles of dimensional measurements.

32.   "Hence, you are to Teach Akh-Hulebuk that the Compass and the Square, are the Tools we Spiritually utilize to Build the Character of MAN, to Travel the 4 dimensions symmetrically.

33.   "These 2 Tools together should symbolize the Spiritual Mentalism-Animating- Navigation manifesting into the visual Character of Solomon in this Natural Molecular-Autonomical-Nucleus here in Nuhfamuoh."

34.   Hotep took the Compass and the Square, and put them together.

And he drew into the ground with his finger, a Circle with 4 Navigational breaks in it; a break North, a break South, a break East and a break West. Centered within the Circle, he drew the number 7. Outside of the Circle, he drew the numbers 9 and 3 and explained their connection to the Circle and 7.

35.   Hotep said unto Baduh: "Teach your portion of Akh-Hulebuk, that the Natural Man should utilize these 2 Tools to establish the base of perpendicular Character, as We are all descendants of Solomon's visual Character, and of the sources of Equational Solutions of the Grand Celestial Government that was ordained by ALLAH the Great Infallible Architect of Mentalism-The Great GOD, Father and Ruler of the Youniverse.

36.   "This Circled 7, at this measurement I convey, symbolizes the Spirit - What we are in Hardcore Reality, manifest in the Natural estate of Solomon, to Build up Nuhfamuoh and the Ark of Hardcore Reality. It is the symbol implying that the Authoritative measurement of Time Governs the manifest Natural Plane, while the Spiritual Mentalism-Animating-Navigation Governs and Masters Time."

37.   Baduh was stung by amazement as he allowed Hotep to enlighten him with such Supreme Education. And he questioned: "Of the rest of these Tools, Hotep- Kebuk, what say you?"

38.   And Hotep said unto him: "Teach Akh-Hulebuk that this Hammer is used to drive in the degree Principles of the dimensional measurements of the Great Infallible Architect of Mentalism.

39.   "To utilize this device, Man must have a sturdy hand, a keen Eye, and precise aim. The proper Time must be taken in the utilization of the Hammer in Character Building, as MAN the Compass develops in stages

of Time measured by the Square.

40. "The nail—being driven by the Hammer, is the Principle; and the Hammer is the driver guided by the labor of MAN.

41. "When used correctly, the Principle will hold the Reality of Everything together. All Hardcore Reality in this instance can be Raised Up as One.

42. "When the Hammer is utilized for this cause, the Natural Estate of MAN will Start to bring Order out of Chaos.

43. "When things are not together, the degree Principles of dimensional measurement are not being driven by a sturdy hand, keen Eye, or precise aim.

44. "This says that the Driver in labor, can't drive the Principles in one pound. The foundation of the drive must be set with easy pounds before the hard pounds are applied. If done in reverse, the Driver can miss the target, dent the product, or damage the Principle.

45. "This Saw is a device used to cut the wood with precision, that every beginning is in harmony with every ending, and the Balance will not sustain damage.

46. "Every Tree picked for Building Shelter is selected by way of its Sturdy Stand, development, health and height. For they make quality Wood to Build with.

47. "This Saw measures every smooth division of Wood in every degree dimensional angle. So shall it Be in Building the Character of MAN.

48. "It makes MAN's Natural ending comply with the Labors taught in MAN's Natural beginnings. They should Be divided by the Saw, in balance, with Smooth Rhythm.

49. "Each stroke is like the Pendulum Swing Rhythmically structured in the Youniverse. No more to one side on the Axis than to the other, in order to maintain smooth results.

50. "This Ax - unlike the Saw, is a device used to chop and not cut. It's designed to bring down the trees in the forest with Force, but not to utilize the Woods for Shelter Building.

51. "The Woods are used for fueling Fires and Building Strength. When Building the Character of MAN, the Ax is used to chop away ungainly parts to strengthen mAN's Force in Nature.

52. "This Plane is a device used to smooth out the Wood, removing all potential kinks that may splinter the Building Blocks.

53. "Uneven kinks in MAN's perceptual visuals in the Consciousness of the Present Moment, represents Chaos in Order, where Light and Darkness are at work in MAN's Thinking at the same time.

54. "Things are not level in MAN's Inner and Outer standings, when the Plane is not utilized to bring Balance to uneven surfaces.

55. "This device also establishes what Plane or degree level MAN functions in, where some may Travel the Planes and stand upon the Axis, while others may only see the Axis from afar in Wonder of its Reality.

56. "For every Character does not Comprehend the established Circumstances of Time's Authoritative measurements; and lo, all of

MAN cannot Be on the same level at the same Time.

57.   "This Chisel is a device used to implement preciseness and definition in the conceptual Consciousness of the Present Moment. With the Hammer, the Chisel knocks away all unnecessary bulk surrounding MAN's endeavors.

58.   "When Building Character, the Chisel is a Molder and should Be delicately used with the pounding drive of the Hammer, the Guiding Eye of MAN and sturdy hand with Creative Touch.

59.   "When Building and Molding Balance in MAN's Character, Chisel away complacency, doubt, fear and imbalanced Standings while delicately imprinting Consciousness of Hardcore Reality.

60.   "The Line is a device used to measure the distance of MAN's Thoughts as they are aligned with the right angle of the Square. The chalk engulfed string - when popped, leaves an imprint of Consciousness at every Level.

61.   "Lines can Be on the Atlas to determine the perpendicularity of Conscious Measurement in Standings or the Axis to determine the level of Consciousness MAN's measurements calculate to.

62.   "We pop the line at MAN's measured degree of Consciousness both perpendicular and on the level, that MAN may have Character to Raise Up through all plights and keep straight the Path of Order.

63.   "This Plummet device is used to determine the Height and Depth of Sound as it is measured from every degree line perpendicular.

64.   "MAN's Character is a Hardcore Mold in Perceptual Reality, built around the Standings in degree on the Square. The Spiritual Mentalism-

Animating- Navigation that is Corresponded In degree Frequencies of Vibration, beholds Mental Sights and Sounds determining perception in the Consciousness of the Present Moment in every degree of Standings.

65.   "At times called the Plumb Line, this device is used to determine where MAN is in Standings to every degree.

66.   "This leads to the 3 Step Ladder. This device is used to climb in Height to Balance Building Blocks for Shelter. When utilized to Build the Character of MAN, the 3 Step Ladder is set on Solid ground that MAN may climb the 3 stages of development in 4 degree dimensional measurements.

67.   "These Stages are the Stairs; these are 3 degrees MAN must climb and travel through in order to Become complete in Character, Comprehension and Circumstances one faces, through/in every step climbed.

68.   "The **1ˢᵗ Step** is Allegiance as a **Student** who will **Learn** the Journey Traveled along the **Way**.

69.   "The **2ⁿᵈ Step** is Confidence as an **Adept-Teacher** who can **Discern** the Signs and Symbols along the path in The Journey Traveled and Stay on course in **Truth**.

70.   "The **3ʳᵈ Step** is **Mastery** of Sight where MAN enters into the Heights to See beyond the Vibrations that calculate slower, beholding the Perfection of the **Light**.

71.   "These Steps are the 3 degrees where MAN's Learning and Discerning transitions into Service for the Building up of the Ark of Hardcore Reality and of Nuhfamuoh. On these 3 Steps, MAN Will Be

Raised Up as a Master of Time.

72. "In this Light, the 12 Step Ladder is the device utilized to Seal the Shelter Built with a cover, as one climbs into the Height of the Sky to stand up on the Seal of Higher ground.

73. "When Building the Character of MAN, every step on the 12 Step Ladder is climbed one step at a Time, in accord with the Teachings from the Sacred Halls of Learning in the Mansions Wheel.

74. "MAN should climb every step to behold the signs given at each Gate, to bring into Nuhfamuoh as Seasonal Cycles, congruent with MAN's Gaining-Obtaining- Developing Motions.

75. "To climb the 12 Step Ladder, MAN must have the Conscious Character that Comprehends the Circumstances presented through the Compass and Square, with Sight of the Symbolic structures of the Circle with the Navigational breaks North, South, East and West, encompassing the 7, and the connections of 3, 9 and 12.

76. "In this manner, structure can Be given to Seasons in accord with MAN's Purpose, meaning, basis and All affairs thereof."

77. And Hotep continued teaching Baduh the symbolic meanings to the Tools given to the Ancient Ancestors of Akh-Hulebuk by Solomon. He unfolded the meanings of the Tools in every degree, and taught Baduh a hieroglyphic style of writing symbolically formed by the Ancestors of Akh-Hulebuk.

78. He wrote out an entire Blue Print stemming from Solomon's Building foundation of Intelligence-Science-Law-Architecture-and-Mathematics, unfolded different degree measures, and gave it All to

Baduh for study, Mastery and Teaching Akh- Hulebuk.

79. Baduh said unto him: "Hotep-Kebuk, your perception of Solomon's Tools and the use of them in Nuhfamuoh, are from a place far from the sensual perceptions of the Ancient Ancestors in Akh-Hulebuk. You are the Fire sent down through Solomon's Seed to help us to know Solomon's Vision.

80. "I will intake this format of Building Character, Comprehension and Circumstance, that I may obey the Fire's request to Teach Akh-Hulebuk the Intelligent-Science-of-Law-Architecture-and Mathematics of internal, esoteric structures of Building Shelters, and the Ark of Hardcore Reality from Solomon's Vision. Should there Be any other things I should know before presenting this to others?"

81. Hotep said to Baduh: "These Lessons will Guide the Akh-Hulebuk Carpenters Guild into the Mental Sight of Creation, Rulership and Government. I will show you how to climb the 12 Step Ladder and see the Council of GODS in the 7 Eyes of ALLAH, The Great I AM, Father and Ruler of the Youniverse.

82. "As ALLAH is The Great I AM - The Great Infallible Architect of Mentalism in the Spiritual Realm, you must Teach Akh-Hulebuk that we will All Raise Up into The Great Infallible Architect of Mentalism in this Natural Realm, and Serve Nuhfamuoh with: the Ark of Hardcore Reality Universities, Sacred Halls of Learning, Temples, Tribes, Government, and bringing Order out of Chaos.

83. **"Baduh, my Natural Father, you are an esteemed Carpenter, Architect, Teacher, Mathematician and mentor here in this element. You are the Sign of the Knowledge of the Council of GODS sent down to give Nuhfamuoh the Seed of Solomon, and**

facilitate Order through Akh-Hulebuk.

84.   "As you convey this portion of Solomon's Vision in its Supreme Stages, the Akh-Hulebuk Carpenters Guild must know that **Solomon never intended for this Order of** Intelligence – Science – Law – Architecture – and - Mathematics **to be a club, Secret Society, covert fraternity, oppressor or any such unrighteous Brotherhood of tyranny.**

85.   "Akh-Hulebuk must Learn to Discern their station of Service. **You must Teach that** Infinite – Sounds – of – Light – that – Animates - Mentalism, **Builds The** Intelligence Science – Law – Architecture – and - Mathematics **of the Coming** Infrastructures – Symbolisms – and – Labors - in our – Ancestral - Morality **in Nuhfamuoh.**

86.   "As you Teach the Carpenters of Akh-Hulebuk how to Master the Tools for this Cause, explain the Seed of Solomon as the Master Teacher of constructing Government, Temples, Tribes, Youniversities, Sacred Halls and Order.

87.   "Teach the All of Man that these Blue Prints that unfolds dimensional degree measurements of ISLAM, are not to Be misused, or kept for Secrets in fraternal structures.

88.   "**Every dimensional degree measurement of ISLAM should not Be seen as Secret. For ALLAH the Great I AM Is the** Involiable Animator of Mastery **of the Youniverse, and All construction therein is Sacred. Each MAN should Learn to Discern MAN that Man may Serve with Purpose and meaning according to the basis.**

89.   "**ISLAM is Order! The Hardcore Reality of ISLAM is the Principle of PEACE. As the Gift of PEACE, I unveil ISLAM as:**

74

Productive – Education – Activating – Cosmic - Energy. **This Intelligent – Science – of – Law – Architecture – and - Mathematics is a** Productive – Education – Activating – Cosmic - Energy. **It is pronounced 'ISLAM' only because its Hardcore Reality spells ISLAM.**

90.   "This is an Order that Teaches the Cosmic National how to Comprehend the established Circumstances of a Generating-Operating-Distributing Character through the Natural Person.

91.   "Akh-Hulebuk must Learn that Nuhfamuoh is the Natural Mother, and All Mentalism- Animating-Navigation is the Sun. Hence, the Carpenters Guild of Akh-Hulebuk must be Raised off of the dead level of complacency, into Living perpendicular Master Masons who are Servants to All Natural Structures of the Natural Mother through the Order of ISLAM.

92.   "Teach the Carpenters Guild to Stand on the Square Within the Circle, as living Perpendicular thereto.

93.   **"Out of this Guild, MAN shall climb the 3 Step Ladder into Mastery and Proclaim the Order of ISLAM: "THE GREAT I AM IS WHAT I AM," From the Height of degree standing into the Depth of degree standing.**

94.   "Verily, verily I say unto you that **I AM -** Hardcore Reality in the Order of Time to bring Balance through the Evolution of Pure Infinite Energy. **I AM - The G**rand – Order - Divine **of the celestial, cosmic expansions here in this terrestrial plane to Serve the Purpose of Gaining** – Obtaining - Developing **Consciousness in Man. I AM - Hotep-Kebuk,** the Spirit MAN of ALLAH The Great I AM, Father and Ruler of the Youniverse, manifest in flesh. **I AM - The** Lawful –

Architectual – Mathematical - Basis of Hardcore Reality.

95. "My Revelation to you is for the Building up of God-Consciousness in Man through the Order of ISLAM. And when you've all reached the right degree measurements, I will reveal more to you in standings for the perpendicular standing of Nuhfamuoh, and the Masonry of Akh-Hulebuk."

96. Baduh and Hotep Built in the Order for Days to come. And it came to pass in the 9th Day, that Mahle came into the Tool shed to check on Hotep. Baduh encouraged him to speak with her.

97. And Hotep said unto Mahle: "Oh Mahle, my Mother Goddess, I AM Kebuk - The Sun of the Mother Principle; Mason. You represent the Gateway into the Natural Plane.

98. "I taught you the contractions and expansions of Holy Breath, as I showed you Solomon's vision of you being a reflection of the Supreme Mother of Natural Metamorphosis. This translates into your Reality being the Womb-of-MAN's Evolution.

99. "You've undergone Metamorphosis and have manifested as the Natural Matriarch of Solomon's Wealth. I've shown you the Fire Waters upon which the Mothership sits. Together we've walked those waters of Unburning Fire, looking within them to see the 24 Elders sitting around the Mountain with the Unburning bush of Fire.

100. "You've taken of the Blue Print to Mothers Building the Universal Temple of Solomon as it was drawn out by the Supreme Mother ISIS - Mother of Natural Metamorphosis, and ate It whole while on the Mothership.

101. "As the Supreme Mother ISIS - Mother of Natural Metamorphosis, walked me through the Mystic chamber called the Plane of Sight, she removed her veil and gave to me the Formula of Natural Solution.

102. "She showed me that you, Mahle, will Teach the surrounding Mothers of Nuhfamuoh that they are, as you are - Builders of the Universal Temple of Solomon in different form.

103. "With you, there's no need for a Hammer, Saw, Ax, Line, or any device that you see before us. You, oh Womb-of-MAN's Evolution, are the Master of Measurements that constructs the transcendental garb for MAN. The Spirit MAN Symbolizes the Compass and you, Mother Goddess, symbolize the Square.

104. "The Womb-of-MAN's Evolution is the Gateway for the Spirit to have entry into Nuhfamuoh in the Male and Female experience.

105. "The Womb-of-MAN's Evolution is symbolic of the Mothership of The SUN, Sailing the Spirit MAN from the Mansions of the Celestial Expansions into the Building grounds in the Natural, where the Youniversal Temple of Solomon is Built without the Sound of a Hammer or ring of any Tool.

106. "As The Cosmic Suns Travel the Journey in the Mothership through the Celestial Seas, they become the Light of the Mother in All terrestrial experience.

107. "Teach surrounding Mothers that you are all Light Bearers of Nuhfamuoh, who will show MAN, **The Way** to **The Truth** of **Light**.

108. "Man cannot see what the Womb of MAN's Evolution is, without

being the SUN of the Mother. I Hotep AM Kebuk, Ma-Mothers-SUN; Hotep-Kebuk, the Light of my Mother; Mason.

109.   "Evolution showed me the Path as I sat on her lap and took of her Nourishment. Infinite Sight Will open the Gates on the Mansions for Intelligent Solution in the terrestrial Plane.

110.   "All Mothers and you, Mahle, Mother Goddess, are the Children of ISIS, as you all have innate abilities to unveil the ship that Journeys through Infinite Seas and sees the Intelligence of Sound vibrate equational Solutions into the Heights and Depths; and you all can carry these Equations and their variables in Great Lengths for measured Widths.

111.   "This dimensional measurement of degrees in 4 expansions and Contractions, begins its Sacred Halls of Learning in 3 stages.

112.   "The **1st Stage** is entry through Dark Matter the Youniversal Mother.

113.   "The **2nd Stage** is entry into the Nourishing Principles of ISIS Squared on All Standings.

114.   "The **3rd Stage** is entry into Nuhfamuoh, the Mother of All Natural Existence.

115.   "I Will Show you the **G**uide-**O**rganizing of this Nation – and - **D**etail **of Constructing Motherships**, if you will follow the vision of Solomon as you so done before I was manifest. Move upon Solomon's perception and you will not sink.

116.   "Mahle and Baduh my Parents in the Natural, Nuhfamuoh will Rise in Wealth, Richness, Grandness and Honor, if you take of these

Tools, Jewels and Divine Instructions, bring them into manifest among the Mothers and the Akh-Hulebuk Carpenters Guild, and contribute to the basis of this cause and its purpose and meaning.

117.   **"The Greatest accomplishment that you can establish is Conscious contribution. There's no Higher degree than Service.**

118.   "To you both, your Purpose in this existence is forth going in Building the Foundation of Nuhfamuoh's Gaining-Obtaining-Developing Consciousness. The start is in the consistency of Raising Up The Lawful-Architectual-Mathematical- Basis of Hardcore Reality.

119.   "Baduh; you will Be the Master Architect, Builder, Carpenter, Engineer, Blue Print Builder and definer of Territories, Temples, Universities, Schools and the Order that will produce Government, Rulership and Supreme Education in Nuhfamuoh Below, as it is in the Celestial Expansions Above.

120.   "Mahle; you will Be the Teacher of Culture, Family, Structure and the Order that Will produce the Teachings of ISIS Unveiled, where All Mothers Will Nurture their Suns from their Breasts With The Formula of Natural Solution.

$$\Longleftarrow \quad O-O-O-O-O \quad \Longrightarrow$$

CHAPTER VII
Hotep Teaches the Order of Paradise and Structures of Building Nuhfamuoh to Buduh's Students

1. And it came to pass, that in Hotep's 28th year into existence within Nuhfamuoh, his development aligned with the Council of GODS variable value, for the Akh-Hulebak Carpenters Guild Gaining Obtaining Developing Consciousness.

2. He taught Mahle the Social, Psychological, Philosophical, Lawful and Mathematical construction of the Mothership, aligning with the Blue Print of ISIS she'd eaten whole in vision.

3. From the Teachings of Hotep, she formed the Mystic School of ISIS, consisting of the Sacred Halls that taught the Womb-of-MAN's Evolution in Nuhfamuoh, the order that comes out of chaos.

4. And the female structure in Nuhfamuoh had their portion of instruction for the Building up of Nuhfamuoh, and the Ark of Hardcore Reality. Comprehension of the established Circumstances came through degree climbing in the Order of Dark Matter, Evolution and Nuhfamuoh.

5. **For All Youniversities, Schools and Sacred Halls of Learning, Hotep established a Curriculum called: Duhah-Nuhle; which was A Know Thyself Curriculum, stemmed from the** Intelligent-Science

of-**L**aw-**A**rchitecture-and **M**athematics.

6.   In The Mystic School of ISIS, The Know Thyself Curriculum taught about the Motions Ruled upon by the Grand Government around The Wheel of Mansions, The Sacred Halls of Learning in the 12 Mansions, the Navigable Waters of the celestial expansions down to the Navigable Waters of Nuhfamuoh, the Supreme Education of Cultivating Nuhfamuoh's SOIL for the Blossoming of I AM, controlling the animals, and Nourishing and Raising Man to be the Stability and Security of, and in the Land.

7.   As it was All Inner Sight, Mothers from the Mystic School of ISIS constructed remedies to every degree for their SUNS in Nuhfamuoh.

8.   **They Became the providers of Nourishing Principles for The Spirit** of **ALLAH**'S - **L**ight and - **L**ove to - **A**ll of - **H**umanity in **M**olecular – **A**utonomical - **N**ucleus.

9.   And The Mothers of Nuhfamuoh were Squared through the Order of Intelligence- Science-Law-Architecture-and-Mathematics.

10.   Baduh was Raised up into the Mastery of Intelligence-Science-Law-Architecture-and-Mathematics. 7 years of Teaching from Hotep gave him the Comprehension of the established Circumstances of Hardcore Reality, the Building of Its Ark, and the Building up of Nuhfamuoh.

11.   He'd started teaching the Akh-Hulebuk Carpenters and Students of Carpentry the Know Thyself Curriculum handed down to him by Hotep, and formed a School surrounding this Architectural vision of Carpentry called: **The Youniversity of ISLAM.**

12.   This Youniversity of ISLAM Taught the Akh-Hulebuk Carpenters

and Students: the dimensional measurements of Character, Comprehension and Circumstances with the Tools that Built quality Temperament, habit and Complexion aligning with the Spiritual Balance of Faluizzi, and Solomon's vision for Nuhfamuoh and the Ark of Hardcore Reality.

13. **From Baduh's vision of Carpentry and Architecture came the Engineering Guild of Operative Masons, that gathered together daily in the Youniversity of ISLAM, Learning in a specific Sacred Hall above the Regular Guild of Akh- Hulebuk. This Sacred Hall of Learning was called: The Architectonic Masonry of Hotep.**

14. As All advanced, Hotep turned 28. He encouraged Baduh to Raise up the Architectonic Masons into The Mastery of ISLAM, in preparation to Serve Nuhfamuoh with the Building of Order.

15. All degrees in the Youniversity formed various Branches in the Akh-Hulebuk Carpenters Guild, with The Architectonic Masonry of Hotep being the Highest.

16. There were Carpenters, Engineers, Architects, Drafting Artists, Linguistic Artists, Stone Cutters and Molders, Constructionists laborers, Pavement layers, Mathematicians, Philosophers, Plumbers, Landscapers, Gardeners, Teachers, Lawmen, Scientists, and Supreme Intellectuals within the Architectonic Masonry.

17. Outside of this Masters Highest degree, the Akh-Hulebuk had Students building up into Adept degrees in the Disciplines of Subject in the Youniversity of ISLAM.

18. And every Man promoted into the Architectonic Masonry of Hotep was recognized as Elders. They All looked to Hotep as their

Spiritual Mensurator.

19.   As Masters of the Craft in every measured degree, Baduh Taught the Elders a Masters Grip, defining them All as Brothers from the Silent Brotherhood of Master Builders in the Architectonic Masonry of Hotep.

20.   **Baduh Taught All Brothers in every degree of The Operative Masonic Guild, to salute one another in a 720° Stance that represented the** Mentalism – Animating - Navigation **from Above, Corresponding with the** Molecular - Autonomical - Nucleus **Below, in Vibrations through the Poles of Negative and Positive charge, in Rhythmic swing of Cause, Purpose and Meanings that defines the basis for All males and females in Nuhfamuoh.**

21.   **He Taught that Man in the Natural Person should salute one another in greetings and departures, standing square - heels together making a vertex, while both feet point out on 45° angles each, making a 90° square on the right angle; left arm down along one's side in a 180° straight angle; right arm squared on the right angle across the chest in a 90° angle with the fingers extended across the heart; head straight forward, aligned with the vertex representing a 360° circle. And With this Salutation, Man should say, ISLAM.**

22.   **And Baduh Taught All Brothers in every degree, the vision of Solomon as it was symbolically structured in two 45° acute angles that formed a square on the right angle, one straight angle in 180°, a square on the right angle of 90° and a circle in 360°. It Was Taught that the salutation represented ALLAH The Great I AM, and Man being One Hardcore Reality.**

23.   Hotep saluted every Elder and then pressed their right hand with

The Masters Grip. And he said unto them: "Elders, Masters and Brothers. You have All been Raised Up into Servants Who Will Service Nuhfamuoh With All degrees of ISLAM. Within this Youniversity, The Light of The WORD constructs disciplines of Subject that raises Man's Standings.

24. "As Masters of The Carpenters Guild, you Elders of Light are to Be henceforth known as the **G**uild – **O**f - **D**edicated - Scholars - **The GODS of Kebuk** in the Natural Order.

25. "You've All Traveled through **I**nfinity – **S**ound – **L**ight - **A**nimation and **M**entalism beyond Faluizzi, and have been granted a copy of the Masters Key to the Portal Doors.

26. "You've elevated through the Sacred Halls of Institutional **A**rchitectural **M**orale in this Youniversity as it is so designed in the Know Thyself Curriculum, and are Brothers in this Silent Brotherhood where your degree of Scholarly, is of Cultivating I AM. **All Elders of this Brotherhood proclaims: I-Self-Law-AM, the Master of the Carpenters Guild.**

27. "Through the Intelligence – Science – Law - Architecture and Mathematics of this Youniversity, The Guild Of Dedicated Scholars Will Build up Nuhfamuoh With Infrastructures – Symbolism – and - Labor in our - Ancestors - Morals.

28. "In Order to Build the Stature, luxury, wealth and Government in Nuhfamuoh as being the Natural estate of MAN, Shelters of Institutional Youniversal Qualification must Be Raised up by WAY of your various skills in Architecture, Ethics, Mathematics, Civics, the various Sciences and All departments of Discipline.

29.   "And these Institutions and Youniversities must withhold the Educational qualifications of the Halls of Learning you've All been through, that it may be seen in Nuhfamuoh's forthcoming Infrastructure-Symbolism-Labor-Ancestry-Morality that will stabilize the People thereof into a **Republic Order of Self Government**.

30.   "All Elders present have climbed the 12 Step Ladder with the Compass and Square and beheld the Governmental Order of Faluizzi with Visual Acuity. You have seen the measurements Time is Master of, and have Raised Up into The Elders degree, I-Self-Law-AM, Master of Time.

31.   "Man that has reached this Masters degree of God-Consciousness is a Master of Time. No Man in this Operative Guild Of Dedicated Scholars can be held down by any Sources of Chaos.

32.   "**ALLAH-The Great** Intelligence of **All M**otion, ordained All things to have structures of Reason, meaning and basis, that Motion may be accelerated in the Balance of Divine Purpose. This was named Order.

33.   "Motion with no bounds is an existence in Nuhfamuoh without Divine Purpose. It is a battle between Light and Darkness as they work at the same time in the same instant with no agreement.

34.   "Consequently, nothing can get done that needs to be fulfilled in the alignment of Divine Purpose. The Thought is Present as The Light, but cannot be brought into manifest due to the distracting shade of the Dark. This was named Chaos.

35.   "Elders, Masters and Brothers of Light, Order is your calling. Time's Authoritative measurements only extend through 4 dimensions. Things bound by Time will begin and end. You as GODS of Supreme

Purpose, Rule Time and any boundless Chaos that may try finding Equality with Order.

36.   "Every Hill and Mountain in Nuhfamuoh is fertile, and ready to receive your structures of Discipline. **I know Nuhfamuoh, she's my Natural Mother.**

37.   "My Supreme Mother of Natural Metamorphosis walked me through the entire land - every inch. I've Traveled across the Fiery Sands—in the distant Northbound area of these grounds where the Bush of Fire that does not Burn, resides upon the Fire Spitting Mountain.

38.   "I've seen the Pyramids, the Monuments, the Temples, the Courts, the Lodges, the Governmental Palace and All Structures you will construct from within the Fiery Sands that are North, all the way to the caves, Mountains and Sharp Rocky grounds that are South of this ground, sit Arithmetically, rise Geometrically and fall Algebraically as Sounds of Light.

39.   "This ground upon which we stand is the Mathematical vertex of Nuhfamuoh, where Time can be calculated according to the Motions of Nuhfamuoh's Gaining Obtaining Developing Order.

40.   "This ground upon which we stand is the Balance of the entirety of the land, where the Red Sea provides drinkable waters throughout the vast expansion.

41.   "In this vast expansion of Nuhfamuoh, there are 7 Hills in total. There are 3 Hills to the North of this vertex, and 3 Hills to the South of this vertex.

42.   "And the Hill on this ground is the area of balance, where MAN

must Be initiated into your order of Infrastructure-Symbolism-Labor-and-Ancestral- Morality.

43. "On this Soil should Stand the Grand Mother Lodge of Executive Governmental Rule, where Man can Gain-Obtain-and-Develop the fundamental basis of Institutional Architectural Morale that leads to the Way to Learning the Truth about The Light.

44. "As there are 7 Hills, there are 7 distinctions of Time measured for Mentalism-Animating-Navigation in this Land. Henceforth, the measurements of Time Will Be deciphered or the like.

45. "Day/Light, and Night/Dark Will Be Seen in the measurements of: Morning, High Noon, After Noon, Evening, Night, Mid Night and Dawn. Man should measure these spans of Time by the Motions of Nuhfamuoh around the Star of Fire.

46. "We Build around these measurements of time and manifest an Executive Governmental Rule By the People in the Evening, a Legislative Governmental Rule Of the People in the Morning, and a Judicial Governmental Rule For The People in the Night.

47. "Everything We Build around this time measurement will fill Nuhfamuoh—from the Fiery Sands North to the Rocky grounds South, where the caves reside."

48. Hotep continued teaching the Elders the Order of Nuhfamuoh's Architectural design. He unveiled the entire Blue Print of Solomon's vision of Orders Standing on the Level, to rise as a living Perpendicular. The Elders were astonished, and anxious to begin.

49. And Hotep concluded: "The Spirit MAN is GOD; GOD to every

degree is a Creator of Paradise in the Natural. As We Build Up Nuhfamuoh, we Will Be Creating Paradise.

50. "Paradise shall Be a manifest representation of Order. Everything will Be left in Legislative file for consistent production of Paradise through Executive Rule.

51. "The descendants of the Elders will one day say: **I will look unto the Hills from whence all help arises as it was established by The Guild Of Dedicated Scholars from the Silent Brotherhood of Master Builders in The Architectonic Masonry of Hotep.**

52. "And lo, our descendants will find Paradise according to our current Conscious Contributions; and the Ark of Hardcore Reality will Be the refuge for All of that measurement of Time, Securing the People from Chaos and Darkness."

53. The Elders All pressed the hands of one another with the Masters Grip, inspired by Hotep's instructions for Building a Paradise that expands through Every Hill and Mountain of Nuhfamuoh.

54. **Hotep stood Square, saluted the Elders and consecutively chanted until the Elders joyfully joined in: The Great I AM is what I AM. THE GREAT I AM IS WHAT I AM; ISLAM! ISLAM! I –** Self – Law - AM, **Master Builder From The SILENT BROTHERHOOD OF ARCHITECTONIC MASONRY, through the Youniversity of ISLAM.**

⇐ O — O — O — O — O ⇒

CHAPTER VIII
The Silent Brotherhood of Master Builders From the Architectonic Masonry of Hotep Establish Infrastructure and Symbolism with Labors Reflecting their Ancestral Morals Throughout Nuhfamuoh

1. And it came to pass, that in the 48th year of existence for Hotep, The Guild Of Dedicated Scholars Built up the estate of Nuhfamuoh in accord with Hotep's perception of Solomon's Blue Print, in variable form from the providence of the Council of GODS.

2. Hotep appointed 7 Elders from the Silent Brotherhood of Architectonic Masonry, as the Foremen of the Ordained project. Each Elder from that time gathered 700 workers in 2 different spans of Day to labor in all Mechanical, Engineering, Architectural procedures drawn out by the Elders **G**uidance – **O**ptimism – and - **D**iagramatical **Formula**.

3. The 2 Shifts of Workers learned on the job, the Wondrous, Motherly

Workings of Nuhfamuoh and her delicacies, intricacies, secrets and wealth.

4. All of Nuhfamuoh was Architecturally drawn into Formulated diagram for Building. Every corner, angle and side was measured and calculated for construction. And the ground in its entirety was dug up.

5. The measurements of the Length of ground dug up—from the 7th to the 1st Hill, was 180,000,000 ft., and its Width was 1,000,000 ft. With this measurement, Nuhfamuoh was divided into 2 Regions along the shores of the Red Sea.

6. Hotep Taught All Master Elders the calculations of Time in accord with Nuhfamuoh's Motions of Gaining-Obtaining-Developing Order. The Balance of The Land was the Divide of the shores of The Red Sea.

7. All lands and grounds North of the shores of The Red Sea were named Upper Nuhfamuoh; and All lands and grounds South of the shores of the Red Sea Were named Lower Nuhfamuoh. And the Red Sea streamed out - both North and South, creating Ponds, Rivers and Lakes throughout the whole of Nuhfamuoh.

8. The Mathematical vertex of Nuhfamuoh was Balanced in the Evening, where the 4th Hill resided. All Hills and Mountains North of the Mathematical vertex were aligned with Hotep's Teachings of Day.

9. In the grounding area of the 5th Hill, the Time of Day was measured and calculated as After Noon, in the grounding area of the 6th Hill, the time of Day was measured and calculated as High Noon. In the grounding area of the 7th Hill, the Time of Day was measured and calculated as Morning. These were All measured by the Motions of Nuhfamuoh when Hotep Traveled through the Sounds of the Winds

with Fire in one hand, and Water in the Other. This became a part of the Architectual design of Nuhfamuoh's Upper Region.

10.   All of the Hills and Mountains South of the Mathematical vertex were aligned with Hotep's Teachings of Night.

11.   In the grounding area of the 3rd Hill, the Time of Night was measured and calculated as Night. In the grounding area of the 2nd Hill, the Time of Night was calculated and measured as Midnight. In the grounding area of the 1st Hill the Time of Night was measured and calculated as Dawn. These were all measured by the Motions of Nuhfamuoh when Hotep Traveled through the Sounds of the Winds with Fire in one hand, and Water in the other. This became a part of the Architectural design of Nuhfamuoh's Lower Region.

12.   The Master Elders unveiled the Mastery of Time in their Blue Print for both Upper and Lower Nuhfamuoh to the laborers.

13.   From the Revelation, the laborers dug deep into the ground, and leveled the bottom surface with tunnels and passages leading from Lower to Upper Nuhfamuoh.

14.   Throughout the entire expansion of 180,000,000 ft, Nuhfamuoh was paved with a road that was broken down into 4 Quarters that withheld 3 Territories.

15.   Two of the Quarters of the Road were in the expansion of Upper Nuhfamuoh; and two of the Quarters of the Road were in the Expansion of Lower Nuhfamuoh.

16.   Standing at the vertex of Nuhfamuoh on the grounds within the area of the 4th **Hill**, the laborers structured **12 distinct columns of**

Pavement.

17.   And right above this portion of the Road, starting from the **5ᵗʰ Hill's grounds**, there were **7 distinct columns of Pavement** with different structure and design that led into the Firey Sands of the 6th and 7th Hills.

18.   And these portions of Road in their differentiations of 12 columns and 7 Columns, were 2 Quarters of the Road paved in the expansion of Upper Nuhfamuoh and its vertex.

19.   Right Below the 2 Quarters of the Road Paved in the expansion of Upper Nuhfamuoh and its vertex, there were **5 distinct columns of pavement** that were relatively larger and wider, extending out along the **grounds of the 3ʳᵈ Hill**.

20.   Below this portion of the Road starting from the **2ⁿᵈ Hill's grounds and extending all the way down to the 1st Hill,** there were **9 distinct columns of Pavement**, that were all connected but broken down in two installments.

21.   There was one installment that was one big sharp Rock paved into 5 columns; and the other, this installment was a much smaller Rock paved into 4 columns.

22.   And these portions of Road in their differentiations of 5 Columns and 9 columns were 2 Quarters of the Road paved in the expansion of Lower Nuhfamuoh.

23.   There were 4 Quarters of Road Paved from the 7ᵗʰ to the 1ˢᵗ Hill. And the Road was called **Gubahu** in Upper and Lower Nuhfamuoh.

24.   There were 3 Territories within the 4 Quarters of Gubahu. The 1ˢᵗ

Territory was throughout the expansion of the 3rd and 4th Quarters of Gubahu and was called: **Ahkeahbuk**.

25.   The Second Territory was throughout the entire expansion of the 2nd Quarter of Gubahu and was called **Ehkeahbu**.

26.   The 3rd Territory was throughout the entire expansion of the 1st Quarter of Gubahu, extending up into the 7th Hill. This was called **Baheleh-yahlu**.

27.   And the Master Elders established this Order in accord with Hotep's Teachings. **Hotep Taught of a Road Paved in 33 columns covered with pearly and silver streets that Man/MAN will Travel in 2 Regional expansions, that measures 7 Time spans throughout 7 Hills in 4 Quarters and 3 Territories**.

28.   He showed them Fire in one hand with Water in the other hand, as the Winds Sounded With the deep vibrations that only the Spirit MAN could hear. And he showed them that the Winds that blew across every Quarter and Territory of the Land would not blow out the Fire, nor spill the Water, if All followed his Supreme instructions.

29.   When MAN Travels through each column in Gubahu, the "I AM" Education, must be acquired by All Natural People from the Student and Adept degrees of the Youniversity of ISLAM.

30.   It was through the Discipline as taught by Hotep, as being a jewel from the Treasure Chest of Solomon that the Consciousness of the Present Moment would harmonize with the vibrations of the Winds— translating the sounds as a Balance between the Water and Fire on the ROAD.

31.   In the underground portion that was all dug up under the silver and pearl covered Road of 33 columns called Gubahu, there was a tunnel that covered the entire 180,000,000 ft. of Land in Length.

32.   The Tunnel had passage ways that gave accessible entry into every portion of Land in Nuhfamouh. This Tunnel was named **Buhuba•**.

33.   On the walls of the Tunnel named Buhuba, inscriptions were chiseled therein, telling a story of the vibrations of the Winds harmonizing with the Consciousness of the Present Moment; and the People from the Guild Of Dedicated Scholars translating All Sound, Traveling and Navigating the Hills and Mountains, Ascending from The Depths into the Heights, and Descending from the Heights into the Depths as the Light of the Word.

34.   Every inch of the Walls told the Story as Hotep Taught the Guild of Dedicated Scholars. It was All chiseled in hieroglyphs and in a language and alphabet designed for Comprehension of Students, Adepts and Noble Masters to every degree from The Youniversity of ISLAM.

35.   At each end of Buhuba, there were stations Built. And the One Built in Upper Nuhfamuoh from the expansion of the 7th Hill was named **Burahu•**, as this was the Central Station Where the Light of the WORD Descended from the Heights into the Depths.

36.   And the one Built in Lower Nuhfamuoh from the expansion of The 1st Hill was named **Buahgu•**, as this was the Central Station where the Perceptual vision of the vibrational Sound of the Winds Ascends from the Depths into the Heights.

37.   These Central Stations in Upper and Lower Buhuba controlled All Lighting functions of Nuhfamuoh.

38.   From the beginning 7 columns of Pavement that started on the grounds of the 5th Hill, down to the beginnings of the rocky grounds around 5 columns of Pavement, there were 31 Light posts built on each side of the Road that illuminated the Land according to measured time.

39.   On both sides of the Road, 31 Light posts together made 62 Lights that Generated Fire throughout Nuhfamuoh's Road.

40.   In front of these Light posts, there were 31 seats for 31 Guards that maintained proper functioning.

41.   On both sides of the Road, 31 Guards together made 62 Guards that maintained proper functioning.

42.   And the 62 guards that maintained proper functioning of the 62 Light posts were 124 Light Bearers in Nuhfamuoh's Road.

43.   At the vertex in the 4th Hills grounds, the Guild Of Dedicated Scholars designed and Built the Grand Mother Lodge of Executive Rule.

44.   Being the Center foundation of the land, it was Built to stand at a Mighty Mile in Height, 500 ft. in Length and 900 ft. in Width. And this Grand Mother Lodge of Executive Rule was named **Ahbuk-Rakebuk**.

45.   This Lodge was the University withholding the Divine Teachings of Intelligence- Science-Law-Architecture-and-Mathematics, opened to The All of Humanity for initiation.

46.   Upon entry, the laborers constructed 3 layers of Walls that the initiate must travel through that were 60 ft. thick each.

47.   All 3 Walls had chiseled within them, signs, symbols and degree messages that the initiate must learn and discern before being qualified

for service with the Guild Of Dedicated Scholars.

48. These Walls were all designed by the Compass, with all hieroglyphic signs, symbols and messages on the Square.

49. And there were great fountains that made water rise and fall throughout Ahbuk-Rakebuk—pumped from the Red Sea, as well as drinking and cleansing fountains from which the initiate must partake.

50. As All 3 Walls were designed in circles, initiates were not to make entry from the 1st Wall into the 2nd or 3rd Walls without having Sound Character to Comprehend the symbolic Circumstances inscribed on the 1st circled wall.

51. There were doors Built within the Walls that could only be opened upon Squaring the Circle. If initiates didn't Comprehend such Circumstances, then the 1st Wall led all back to the beginning entry doors for initiates to restart the initiation process.

52. Traveling through the 3 layers of walls was Taught by Hotep, as being Nourished by The Mother of Natural Metamorphosis Where, Intelligent Solutions are learned through a Plane of Infinite Sight on the Journey. It symbolized sitting on the knee of ISIS as an Infant, sucking the Formula from her Breast.

53. And the 3 walls symbolized the 3 degrees that makes 360 degrees All initiates must travel through on the 3 Step Ladder. This portion of Ahbuk – Rakebuk - as an initiation phase, was called **Lubukmah**.

54. Each wall had a name. The **1st Wall** was called **The Wall of Lehe**, the **2nd Wall** was called **the Wall of Keoh**; the **3rd wall** was called **The Wall of Lemu**.

55. Lubukmah was designed in the order of the Compass. Upon passing the Wall of Lemu, there was a fountain where All initiates cleansed the body in preparation for the next Built phase of Ahbuk-Rakebuk.

56. And lo, designed by the Square, there was a Building within Ahbuk-Rakebuk that had 4 Halls, connected to 2 Massive Assembly Courts, one on each side of Ahbuk-Rakebuk.

57. 2 of the Halls were Upper Rooms called **Mother Chambers,** where the initates enter to be cleansed by the Great Heights of Sight; and 2 of the Halls were **Lower Rooms,** where initiates expand in existence as GOD in flesh.

58. The **Assembly Courts** surrounding Ahbuk-Rakebuk were entered by initiates in silence, as the Development of Pure Infinite Thoughts from ALLAH The Great Infallible Architect of Mentalism echoed throughout.

59. In silence, initiates release any and all vain Thoughts, and learn the sounds of the winds with Fire in one hand and Water in the other.

60. When the Pure Infinite Thought that Travels as the vibrational sound of the Wind is translated, the initiates are led through Double Doors called **The Doors of Renewal,** where there are 2 separate flights of stairs.

61. One flight leads the Way into lower Nuhfamuoh, and the other flight leads the way into Upper Nuhfamuoh.

62. On the Walls leading to both destinations, there were stories told in hieroglyphic form, explaining Hotep's Journey Traveled through the very

same system.

63.   And the flight of stairs that led the Way into Upper Nuhfamuoh, gave the initiate the opportunity to go within the **Sacred Room** atop the Building of 4 Halls.

64.   When the hieroglyphic story of Hotep's Journey Traveled was Comprehended, All initiates were able to see the Door on the wall leading to another flight of stairs that led to a Sacred Rocm Holding **the Arc of Ahbuk-Rakebuk's Order.**

65.   And it was after being exposed to the Arc of Ahbuk-Rakebuk's Order, that All initiates were faced with Circumstances of Executive Rule.

66.   And the flight of stairs that led the Way into Lower Nuhfamuoh gave the initiates access into the Judicial Halls and Courts, that were stationed in the 3rd Hill.

67.   And this was the Grand Mother Lodge that resided in the vertex of Nuhfamuoh on the grounds of the 4th Hill.

68.   Surrounding the Assembly Courts and Ahbuk-Rakebuk, there were **12 Pearly Gate Posts** on each side of the Road, leading down and angled squarely with the 12 Columns of Pavement.

69.   A ceiling was designed in 3 installments connecting 7 posts of the 12, on each side of the Road.

70.   The Land in the 4th Hill surrounding the 12 columns of Pavement, in the Ehkeahbu Territory was called: **Kerafa,** as it was the Matriarchal Land of GODS Order. And this was the 2nd Quarter parcel to the vertex of Nuhfamuoh's Executive Rule By the People.

71.   In the 3rd Quarter parcel to Lower Nuhfamuoh within the Land of the 3rd Hill surrounding the 5 columns of pavement in the Ahkeahbuk Territory, there was an entirely different Rule of Order structured.

72.   Everything Built by the Guild Of Dedicated Scholars in Lower Nuhfamuoh dealt in the Business structures For the People of Nuhfamuoh.

73.   And the Judicial Administration had the permission of establishment For the People, By the People of Nuhfamuoh, with the authoritative power to interpret all Legislative Rule that consisted of the People of Nuhfamuoh's Natural Law, as constructed into the Sovereign Authority of the entirety of the Land.

74.   The Judicial Administration was granted permission from the Legislative Rule Of the People, to translate from All Natural Law, a means of creating Business, labor, mercantile, markets, merchandise, and dealings of employment.

75.   The Judicial Administration made up a legal system that only applied in/to the Business structure of Nuhfamuoh. All statutes, codes, ordinances, protocols, and provisions, were a part of the legal system of Nuhfamuoh, that had its permission of a Business existence and establishment, through All Legislative Rule of the People and All Executive Rule By the People.

76.   The Judicial Administration knew that they were not the Law; they knew that their authoritative power extended only as interpreters of Natural Law, to make **legal - not Lawful Order,** into Business Structure For The People.

77.   There were 9 Judges that made up the Judicial Administration. The

Administration Building was Built on the first 2 columns of Pavement in the 3rd Hill.

78.   2 Court Buildings were Raised up, with the Highest level floors being Administrative. They were oval shaped and sat on the ends of the Road.

79.   Great corporate Buildings, infrastructures, Businesses and schools of legal order were Constructed employing the People of Nuhfamuoh with work for wages.

80.   And the Judicial Administrations venue extended from the 3rd Hill throughout Lower Nuhfamuoh.

81.   Hotep ordered 3 specific functions for the steady development of the Judicial Power. The 1st was proper legal order for the corporate venue, the 2nd was proper legal order for all commercial wages, created and distributed to the People for work and living, and the 3rd was proper legal order for All Business establishments.

82.   There were 3 stations in the Administrative power that governed the orders as given by Hotep. The **1st** was called **the Station of Bahelebu**, the **2nd** was called **The Station of Balukeeh**, and the **3rd** was called **The Station of Bukguleh.**

83.   The Land in the 3rd Hill surrounding the 5 columns of pavement in the Ahkeahbuk Territory was called **Rahunuh**, as it was the Government of Commercial Business. And this was the 3rd Quarter, parcel to Lower Nuhfamuoh.

84.   In the 4th Quarter, parcel to Lower Nuhfamuoh, within the Land of the 2nd Hill surrounding the 5 columns of pavement in the Ahkeahbuk

Territory, there was an enormous Rock covering the entirety of the 5 columns of pavement.

85. The Guild Of Dedicated Scholars had the laborers dig into the Rock, until caves with tunnels of entry and exit were present.

86. Within the caves, hieroglyphs were engraved into the walls as signs of Light shining in the Dark of the Night.

87. Passage Ways were made, that the caves may Be climbed and entered by All working the grounds.

88. Around the enormous Rock of Caves, there was a **borough** parcel to the Judicial Administrations venue, designed in the form of a **degenerate skull**.

89. On the grounds thereof, consisted everything from Think tanks for Business, to Shelters, to tunnels that led the way into Upper Nuhfamuoh.

90. This ground extended all the way beyond the 1st Hill forming the **Arc of Heah**.

91. And All Business extended throughout the Land surrounding the 5 columns of Pavement, in the form of a degenerate skull.

92. The Land in the 2nd Hill surrounding the 5 columns of pavement in the Ahkeahubk Territory was called **Hubale**, as it was the Land of Commercial Subordinate Enterprises.

93. South of the enormous Rock and Caves in the 1st Hill, there was a small Rock with 4 columns of Pavement surrounding it.

94. The Guild Of Dedicated Scholars had their Laborers dig 2 caves

into the Rock. These Caves withheld tunnels that had entry, one into the other.

95.   At the end of the 4th Column, there were 2 more Lights with 2 more Guards on each side of the Road. That made **33 Lights and 33 guards on each side of the Road**.

96.   And there were 132 Light Bearers throughout Nuhfamuoh maintaining proper functioning and Order. Throughout the land with the Guards and Lights, the Order of Hotep was maintained. The 2 Lights and 2 guards on each side of the Road of the 4th column proved the Dawn to be a spawn of Day.

97.   On the land in the 1st Hill, there was a great medical facility Raised up that gave Man the education to harvest the ground, plant within the soil, and protect the harvest with the medicines designed by Hotep.

98.   The Land in the 1st Hill surrounding the 4 columns of Pavement in the Ahkeahbuk Territory was called **Kelehba,** as it was Man's facility teaching the Nurturing of planting and harvesting the ground, and injecting the proper medicines therein.

99.   And this was the Building up of the land throughout Lower Nuhfamuoh in the 3rd and 4th Quarters of the Ahkeahbuk Territory.

100.   In the 1st Quarter parcel to Upper Nuhfamuoh, the venue was of a Legislative Rule Of the People. All Natural Laws were of a Legislative document for file and Governed the affairs of All Judicial and Executive Rule.

101.   Hotep explained to the Guild Of Dedicated Scholars, the seemingly immaterial abode of Nothingness withholding Immortality that

is Everything.

102. The Master Builders watched Hotep gather a handful of sand, form from it with waters, a bird, and Breathe the Holy Breath into it. He then spoke to it according to the Arithmetical base, the Geometric Rise and dry misty Fall of Algebraic sand tides.

103. From this Reality, the bird manifested into existence, and flew away into the Heights of the Ether plane.

104. The Master Elders Learned from Hotep the Mastery of Creation as the teaching surrounded Nuhfamuoh, only being alive through their Raising Her up, and speaking her grounds into existence with the Holy Breath.

105. And lo, the Guild Of Dedicated Scholars took from the High degree, the Blue Print to the Building of The Legislative Rule of Upper Nuhfamuoh.

106. On the 5th Hill surrounding the 7 Columns of Pavement in the Baheleh-yahlu Territory, a school was Built that taught of Nutrition and medicines, that dealt in cleaning the drinking waters of the Red Sea, and dealt in manufacturing the mix of chemicals that kept the solid ground durable.

107. And the school was a Great Building of 2 stories. The Top Story had 2 Upper Rooms and the Surface had 2 Lower Rooms.

108. Around this School was Built Energy Centers on which Solar Energy illumined. Atop the Great Building, there was a small pyramid built that generated most of its power in the Afternoon. This School was called **Lueh-Rabumu.**

109.   North of this School, there was Built an Altar where the People of Nuhfamuoh could get on their knees and concentrate on the Law in reverence to Father ALLAH the Great I AM.

110.   Hotep taught out front, the Guild Of Dedicated Scholars how the Consciousness of the Present Moment held within a Sound that could Be heard throughout the expansion of Faluizzi; it was the WORD in Motion.

111.   All who kneel on the Altar, must do so in silence with the sincerity of concentration on Natural Law; and All who done so, visions were heard by the Great I AM, as the Sound of vision vibrated at a frequency that projected beyond sight.

112.   These felt while unseen vibrations were called partners of the winds, as they had the power to create through the Order of Natural Law, and exist beyond visual measurements.

113.   And the Altar was called **Buklehex** in the Day it was Built, named by Hotep.

114.   Right next to the Altar of Buklehex, there was a Great Carpet rolled out extending far in the land of the 5th Hill. On it was only allowed Master Builders that spoke Law into Order and rationalized Reality one to another.

115.   The Carpet was Sacred, and apart of the Buklehex Altar. All had to remove their shoes before touching it.

116.   **Hotep broke the Carpet down into 3 Sections. The 1st was called Bukra- Akhlehle, as this was the portion where All Vibrational Sound that was felt while unseen as the Winds, was**

secured into Rational Order for the Reality of Natural Law.

117. The **2ⁿᵈ was called Ehohmu,** as this was the portion where Rational Order became Mathematical calculations jotted down for variable movements that worked out the sounds of vibration into the manifest of existence.

118. The **3ʳᵈ was called Baluoh,** as this was the portion where variables of Mathematical Motions of Sound, were solved and pinpointed into the Natural Order of Law.

119. **Hotep constructed 3 steps on the Masters Carpet** for the Noble Master Elders of Nuhfamuoh, that they may teach in the Youniversity of ISLAM, how to learn and discern that they may all become Masters, who will Serve Nuhfamuoh through felt but unseen vibrations that partners up with the winds.

120. And the Masters Carpet in conjunction with the **Altar called Buklehex was called Lurale**.

121. North of that site on the 2nd Column of Pavement, there was an Island on the level pointing East and West. On this Island, all of the Master Builders had the Laborers construct telescopes where the expansion of the Governmental Palace could be seen from East to West.

122. On this Island, MAN was to concentrate to see the Negative and Positive ends of the Law Pole through Inner and Outer Standings.

123. The Level was engraved into the Pavement ground of the 2nd Column; and this was called the Axis Island.

124. On the 1ˢᵗ column of Pavement, there was another Island pointing North and South. On this Island, the Master Builders had the laborers

construct telescopes where the expansion of the Governmental Palace could Be seen from North to South.

125. On this Island, the Spirit MAN Was to concentrate on what was seen on the Negative and Positive fields at the ends of the Law Pole, and construct Comprehension of All Circumstances from the Greatest Heights into the profound Depths of Over and Under Standings.

126. The Plummet was engraved into the Pavement of the 1st Column in the 5th Hill; and this was called Atlas Island.

127. From the Atlas Island, the coordinate system of the Governmental Palace could Be seen Geometrically Rising and Algebraically falling upon an Arithmetical setting. From the Axis Island, both the Inner and Outer Workings of the Governmental Palace stood sound in the Consciousness of the Present Moment.

128. This Atlas Island had a **canal** that stretched out in mass proportion connected to the **Hubaakh River,** which extended into the Oceans of the 6th and 7th Hill, on down to the 1st Hill.

129. The canal started from the Atlas Island, and extended into the **Akhlueh-Gulebu Lake** of the 5th Hill. And there was a **Bridge** Built from the Atlas Island going North into the **Ground of Monuments,** which was the **1st of 3 tracts** in the Land surrounding the 6th Hill.

130. And this Bridge was called **Nuhlehbu-Baluke,** as it was the walkway over the canal into the Grounds withholding Monumental Artifacts in the 6th Hill.

131. And the Land in the 5th Hill parcel to the Baheleh-yahlu Territory in Upper Nuhfamuoh was called **Buknuhyah,** as it was the land with

great Islands and Bridges.

132.   Across the Nuhlehbu-Baluke Bridge was the 1st Tract of land in the 6th Hill. This was a land holding Monumental Artifacts designed by Hotep and the Master Builders.

133.   This 1st tract was called **Lehlubu-Huheex** by the Master Elders, as it was the Grand entry into the 6th Hill.

134.   At the exit way of the Nuhlehbu-Baluke Bridge, there was a Legislative Building that was designed to keep the initiate's records in file for Governmental notification.

135.   This Building held Executive documents of All initiates Traveling through Ahbuk-Rakebuk, and all progress reports from there, to the current degree standings.

136.   All initiates had to register their standing degree into the Record before being granted entry into Lehlubu-Huheex.

137.   Once the initiates were identified, they were led into a room to purify, and then go through a tunnel door that led the way into an unknown location within Buhuba.

138.   Initiates were to read the hieroglyphs that will lead the Way, from deep within the underground into the **Pyramids**.

139.   From deep within the underground, the Pyraminds were Built from Top to Bottom - the top being the deep layers, passages and levels underground; the bottom being the surface of upperground. And from that point, the Pyramids were Built from Bottom to Top.

140.   There were 2 Great Monumental Pyramids that were illuminated

by the Fire in the Sky at High Noon; one on each side of the road.

141. Initiates had to find their way out of the Pyramids, by Comprehending the meanings of their inner workings and messages conveyed hieroglyphically.

142. Finding the way out, dealt in the Initiates Learning the balance between the Morning and High Noon, as the Pyramids were Built and stationed in such an accord.

143. Once Initiates found the Way out of the Pyramids, there was seen **2 Monumental Rocks** - one on each side of a Pyramid. They were massive, and **sculpted into Faces**.

144. Hotep taught of these Great Faces on the sides of the Pyramids as proof of order in High Noon. These Great Monumental Rocks were called **Faguba**.

145. The initiates pass Faguba, and follow the Road into a **Great Meeting Hall**—where all Legislative Law is Learned and constructed into the harmony of Thinking, Feeling and Will.

146. The initiates Learn to Discern the Balance as the Spirit MAN conjuncted with the Natural Man. There were many Rooms the initiates traveled through, to develop the Comprehension of the Circumstances of All-Law.

147. This Great Meeting Hall was a Monumental Artifact called **Hulehnuh-bukke**.

148. Centering the Pyramids outside of Hulehnuh-bukke, there was a **Gigantic Tree** that was like no others; and it grew in All seasons providing the Proper Shade in the High Noon expansion.

149.   The fruit of this tree had the energy from the Fire in the Sky, producing strength, alertness and zeal to initiates upon Consumption that the Journey traveled may stay consistent in the Light of Day.

150.   It was called **the Tree of The Knowledge of Conscious Power;** and it was deemed Wise to take of its fruit.

151.   Once the initiates pass the Tree of the Knowledge of Conscious Power, there lied another **Great Bridge** with hieroglyphs chiseled in every area.

152.   This Bridge had a Root over it; and it led into the 2nd Tract called **Buknuhhu-Baoh**. And the Bridge was called **the Hebuba Bridge**.

153.   In Buknuhhu-Baoh, there was a **Garden** withholding many plants, trees and stations of Legislative Order. This was called **the Garden of Faheleh-lubu**.

154.   The Hebuba Bridge led the way; **2 small trees** were on each side of it. The trees were like bushes that produced berries that gave initiates the ability to see the Light of the WORD. They were called **the Trees of Vision**.

155.   Initiates were to eat of the tree's berries, and walk through the Garden.

156.   And there were many Trees that produced various sources of substance for initiates to partake from, implying that Paradise was its source of existence.

157.   Deep into the Garden, there were **2 Great Onyx Stones** that Hotep taught fell from the sky, and operates the energy filled produce

through the soil of the ground in the Garden of Faheleh-lubu.

158.   They were impenetrable, and could not be chiseled. Hotep taught of their inner materials being of the Cosmic Mother's Dark Matter, and that they were Nuhfamuoh's Birth Marks.

159.   These stones were called **Bazinuh-Buyahra**. All Initiates were to touch the **Onyx/Black Stones,** and allow their electrical currents to operate on All inner parts.

160.   Once out of the Garden, there was an Assembly Dome where All Legislators voted on Laws for Nuhfamuoh's advancement. North of Lulehmu-Gulebu's beginning, the **Assembly Dome** was Built atop this Great Lake and Was called **the Luehkeba Dome**.

161.   It spreaded long, and stayed occupied with Workings for Nuhfamuoh's advancement.

162.   Just West of the Luehkeba Dome, there was a **Laboratory** where Legislative Scientists strictly dealt in the internal functions of the Natural man's motions. And this Labratory was called **Ehhelu-ehbuk**.

163.   Within Ehhelu-ehbuk, there were **Rooms** where initiates can see within Hardcore Reality, and learn to discern its Psychometric Mathematical base. These Rooms were called **Keahke-nuhmule**.

164.   Beyond Ehhelu-ehbuk Labratory, there was the Legislative **House of Order** where, the Operation of Nuhfamuoh was constructed into All-Law.

165.   There were 2 offices in the small House of Order that dealt in all major functions in the Legislative, Executive and Judical Rules. And this Legislative House of Order was called **Heyahlu-Rabukmu**.

166. Slightly South of this Great House, there was a Legislative **Law Library called Ehyahhe-Huahke**. This Library had an **Upper level** only for Masters; and it was called **Akhlehluex**.

167. And this was the 2nd Tract in the 6th Hill in the Baheleh-yahlu Territory, parcel to Upper Nuhfamuoh in the 1st Quarter.

168. Hotep layed out a special Blueprint for the 3rd Tract, as it consisted of the 7th Hill and the Legislative Governmental Palace.

169. And it was Taught to All Master Builders that the 3rd Tract portion of Nuhfamuoh, was the most Sacred of the estate, and shouldn't be altered in its Natural position.

170. Hotep Taught of the grounds in the 7th Hill, being walking grounds of ALLAH the Great I AM; as the Mountain surrounding the 7th Hill was illuminated by ALLAH'S presence.

171. Upon the Mountain in the 7th Hill, there was a Bush that appeared to Be on Fire, but did not burn. It illuminated the top portion of the Mountain with a Radiant Glow, as the Morning illuminated the 7th Hill.

172. Hotep explained to the Master Builders that only they themselves—as the Silent Brotherhood of Master Builders in the Arcitectonic Order of Masonry could Build up the estate of the 3rd Tract in the land of the 7th Hill, and the Ark of Hardcore Reality.

173. Hotep also explained that the Sacred grounds holding the unburning Fire, were not to Be touched until Comprehended, and that the unburning Fire was the Light of the WORD of ALLAH that led to the portal doors beyond Nuhfamuoh's expansion into Faluizzi and beyond.

174. Hotep himself climbed the Mountain in the 7th Hill, and Built a Throne behind the Burning Bush that did not Burn and a panel door post around it.

175. And he chiseled the Pass Word:

Keahbu-Dūhāh-Nuhlē/⊢ ⌂ ,

in the top door post along with Building a small box in which he put a copy of the Masters Key.

176. The Mountain was not accessible to initiates that were not promoted into Service of the Guild Of Dedicated Scholars. Hotep called this Mountain **The Heyahbu-leahbuk Mountain** in the Day that he Built the Throne.

177. And he Taught that the Throne Implied that All Authority, All Power and ALL Rulership in Nuhfamuoh, was through the Supreme Force of ALLAH The Great I AM. All Master Elders knew that the Order of Proclamation was intertwined in the Pass Word Where, ALLAH the Great I AM and Man in the Youniversity of ISLAM are One.

178. None who lacked Comprehension of the Proclaimed Order, the Great I AM is what I AM, were permitted into the 7th Hill, nor the Heyahbu-leahbuk Mountain where Hotep placed the Master Key, the Throne, the Doer Post with the Pass Word and the Blue Print to the Building of the Ark of Hardcore Reality.

179. North of the Heyahbu-leahbuk Mountain was the **3rd Tract** that was called **Hulenuh-Huluex**. In this tract was the land of the 7th Hill.

180. Surrounding the Heyahbu-leahbuk Mountain was the **Governmental Palace** of Legislative Rule. It was a castle like luxury involving the Master Builders Chambers of High degree Order of Operation.

181. The Palace consisted of 4 Sacred Walls that made up the outskirts and Roof of the Building Structure. In the Walls the Pure Infinite Energy of Hardcore Reality was present.

182. The sands surrounding the Governmental Palace of Legislative Rule, were Burning with the unburning Fire of Hardcore Reality and Pure Infinite Energy of God-Consciousness; and they were very well alive in Nuhfamuoh.

183. The Wall Built behind the Heyahbu-leahbuk Mountain was called the **Fahuhelu Wall**. And there was a Building made by the wall that had the Masters Chambers of Legislative translation.

184. The wall Built juxtaposed to the Heyahbu-leahbuk Mountain was called the **Lukehe Wall**. And East to West there was a Building made by the Wall that had the Masters Chambers of Supreme Character that had a Divine Sense of Comprehending Legislative Circumstances.

185. The Wall that was the Roof of the Palace was called **the Helehlu Wall**. And there was a ceiling covering the Wall with Art that showed Nuhfamuoh, as a Beautiful Womb-of-MAN's Evolution being Raised off a dead level into the living Perpendicular Mother of the Natural Metamorphosis of Man.

186. The Art told a story of her becoming and giving Birth to the Natural Man, descended from Solomon, descended from Atom and Evolution, that Raised up Hotep-Kebuk. The ceiling was a Masters

Chamber of Legislative calculations of Psychometric Mathematical Equational Solutions.

187.   The Wall Built in front of the Heyahbu-leahbuk Mountain was called **the Akhlehlu Wall**. And there was a Building made by the wall that had the Masters Chambers of Legislative traveling where all Master Elders utilized the Masters key, to open the Portal doors and travel the unlimited expansions of Hardcore Reality.

188.   The Governmental Palace of Legislative Rule was called **Rafagu-Heahbuk**.

189.   On the West side of the 7th Hill in a 180° curve, there were 12 Thrones surrounding the One Throne on the Heyahbu-leahbuk Mountain, with 12 Master Elders Seated in them.

190.   On the East side of the 7th Hill in a 180° curve, there were 12 Thrones surrounding the One Throne on the Heyahbu-leahbuk Mountain, with 12 Master Elders seated in them.

191.   **And there were 24 Elders on 24 Thrones surrounding the One Throne of ALLAH the Great I AM, enclosed by 4 sacred walls in the 3rd Tract and 3rd Territory of Baheleh-yahlu.**

192.   **The design represented the Compass and the Square, that makes the circled 7.**

193.   The Whole of Nuhfamuoh was Built up in Balance Surrounding Rafagu-Heahbuk. There were twin oceans called **the Bukahlu-Gulebu Oceans.** From the Subordinate areas extended West, East and South of the Gubahu Road, Nuhfamuoh was Built standing as a Living Perpendicular on the Square.

194.   And When Order was established throughout Nuhfamuoh, Hotep was burying both Mahle and Baduh who had changed forms. And he was 48 years into existence when entombing his Natural Parent's remains in the caves of the 1st Hill.

195.   Hotep Became the Official Successor of Solomon over the Akh-Hulebuk Carpenters Guild, and the Silent Brotherhood of Master Builders form the Architectonic Order of Masonry.

196.   He assured the Master Elders that the Ark of Hardcore Reality would Be Built by them upon his departure from Nuhfamuoh.

197.   And the People of Nuhfamuoh deemed Hotep Ruler of All Structures of Rulership; but he assured them all that ALLAH the Great I AM Is the Father and Ruler of All things, and that having Character to Comprehend the Circumstances of the Proclamation: The Great I AM is what I AM will make ALLAH and Man ONE. He also assured them that All Structures of Rulership were Built for MAN to Know Man/Self, and for MAN to be GOD the Ruler of the Youniverse.

198.   Nuhfamuoh Became a Wealthy and prosperous Order of Balance. Order was Brought out of Chaos and All-Law Governed the Affairs of the estate.

199.   Things advanced, as Gaining Obtaining and Developing Became the leading ideal motion of Culture. From the 1st to the 7th Hill - and All Subordinate areas, the All of Nuhfamuoh was on the Square in All Standings.

200.   And this was the Infrastructure - Symbolism - Labor - Ancestral vision and – Morality, All constructed into the Supreme Order of Nuhfamuoh. Hotep and the Master Elders elected officials for every

Governmental Station of Rule, to begin the High degree service of Nuhfamuoh's functioning. They toured the entirety of the land; and All was Well and in accord with Solomon's vision.

$$\Longleftarrow \quad O-O-O-O-O \quad \Longrightarrow$$

CHAPTER IX
Hotep Teaches the Principles of Law in Ahbuk-Rakebuk to the Executive Order of Rule

1. Nuhfamuoh was Raised Up into Order by the Guild Of Dedicated Scholars. All things were prosperous throughout both regions as The People obeyed the Law.

2. Accordingly, The People of Nuhfamuoh branched off into Tribes throughout the 7 Hills and 3 Territories. There were 7 Tribes that inhabited the Land and dealt in the prosperity therein.

3. And the 1st Tribe of the Lower Region in the 4th Quarter of the Ahkeahbuk Territory was called the Ahba Tribe. The 2nd Tribe of the Lower Region in the 3rd Quarter of the Ahkeahbk Territory was called the Lehunuh Tribe.

4. And the 3rd Tribe of the Lower Region in the 3rd Quarter of the Ahkeahbuk Territory was called The Kehufa Tribe. These were the tribes that inhabited the first 3 Hills of the 3rd and 4th Quarters of the Ahkeahbuk Territory parcel to the Lower Region of Nuhfamuoh.

5. The People of the Tribes in the Ahkeahbuk Territory were initiated into the Order of ISLAM and became Merchants of Commercial Order, the Employers of Commercial Business governed by the Legal System of Judicial Rule and Agricultural Scientists. They shined Light in the Night.

6. And the 4th Tribe of the vertex of Nuhfamuoh in the 2nd Quarter of the Ehkeahbu Territory was called The Ahbukyah Tribe. Hotep Taught of this Tribe as being the facilitating Balance of All Tribes, and called the Ahbukyah Tribe the ALI Tribe.

7. The Ahbunkyah/ALI Tribe were the only inhabitors of the 2nd Quarter of the Ehkeahub Territory. They were mainly the Akh-Hulebuk Carpenters Guild; and they were raised up by Hotep to Shine as ALLAH'S Light of ISLAM.

8. And the 5th Tribe of the Upper Region in the 1st Quarter of the Baheleh-yahlu Territory was called the Bazi Tribe. The 6th Tribe of the Upper Region in the 1st Quarter of the Baheleh-yahlu Territory was called the Rabukleh Tribe.

9. And the 7th Tribe of Upper Nuhfamuoh in the 1st Quarter of the Baheleh-yahlu Territory was called the Bumahzi Tribe. These were the Tribes that inhabited the last 3 Hills of the 1st Quarter of the Baheleh-yahlu Territory parcel to the Upper Region of Nuhfamuoh.

10. The People of the Tribes in the Bahleh-yahlu Territory were graduates of the Youniversity of ISLAM, and were Masons in the High degrees of ISLAM'S Order. They were Teachers and Masters from the Architectonic Masonic Structure.

11. These Master Builders and Teachers of ISLAM were the Guild Of Dedicated Scholars making up the Silent Brotherhood; and they were able to discern the Sounds of the Youniverse pour out in high frequency vibrations. They were Supreme Governors of the Legislative Rule and were holders of the Masters Key, fully capable of Navigating through the Womb of the Youniverse. They Ruled In the Day.

12.   Hotep had the Master Builders construct 7 Temples/Lodges in the 7 Hills to enlighten the Youth of the 7 tribes, about the Order that comes out of Chaos.

13.   In the 4th Hill, There was constructed the Temple/Lodge of ALI, as ALLAH'S Light of ISLAM shined as the Balance and Order of Nuhfamuoh.

14.   In the 3rd Hill there was constructed the Temple/Lodge of AL, as this was the territory where the Judicial Administration established a Legal System descended from the Legislative Rule.

15.   In the 2nd Hill there was constructed the Temple/Lodge of DEY, as the People shined the Light of Day in the Region of the Night.

16.   In the 1st Hill there was constructed the Temple/Lodge of EL as the People were creators and definers of Order.

17.   In the 5th Hill there was constructed the Temple/Lodge of MOOR, as the Mentalism Of Order Ruled and Navigated through All frequencies of Sound, translating harmony and Thought.

18.   In the 6th Hill there was constructed the Temple/Lodge of BEY, as the Grand Body of GODS Governed as well as Obeyed All-Law.

19.   In the 7th Hill there was constructed the Temple/Lodge of ALLAH, where only Master Masons were permitted as Hardcore Reality was revealed.

20.   And Hotep was 70 years into existence when Nuhfamuoh's 7 Temples stood as Teaching Lodges for the youth of the People.

21.   All-Law was documented into Legislative file and enforced through

the Executive Order. Nuhfamuoh stood perpendicular.

22. In the Evening, Hotep met with the Executive Board in Ahbuk-Rakebuk. He taught the Executive Order the Principles of Reality.

23. And he said unto them: "My People, I AM now in the ranks of an Elder and my Natural Strength is on the decline. As Nuhfamuoh stands today by the construction of Infrastructures-Symbolism-and Labors-with-Ancestral-Morality, so shall it continue to stand and live as the Mother of the Natural People.

24. "I Will not Be around much longer. Comprehend the Circumstances of this vision I will unfold to you that you may maintain your Executive Standings on the Square.

25. "There's no Higher degree established for Man than Service. Subsequent to Learning the Way and Discerning the Truth, Man walks in the Light as a Servant to Nuhfamuoh.

26. "Verily verily I say unto you - The Executive Order, that your station in this Government Of Dominion is to keep Order in the bounds of what's Right.

27. "For the Executive Rule is the **G**enerator of Order. The Legislative Rule is the **O**perator of All-Law and the Judicial Rule is the **D**istributer of Economic Wealth. The People are the Source of the Power of All 3 Rules; and All 3 Rules in this accord is the Natural GOD.

28. "It is the responsibility of this station to serve Nuhfamuoh with perpendicular Principles, that the Mother and Her Suns may continue to prosper when I depart.

29. "The Hardcore Reality of MAN is One; this is Law. The expansion

122

of the Hardcore Reality of MAN is TWO. The Natural Order of the Hardcore Reality of Man is Three.

30.   "The One, is the Spiritual Mentalism-Animating-Navigation, and is the Hardcore Realist. The Two is the Spiritual Mentalism-Animating-Navigation in conjunction with the Consciousness of the Present Moment. This is the Soul- Of-Man, or Mind and Soul. The Three is the Spiritual Mentalism-Animating- Navigation within the transcendental vehicle of Consciousness/Soul, within the Natural Molecular-Autonomical-Nucleus, this is Mind-Soul-and-Body or Spirit- Conscious -Matter.

31.   "This Threefold Construction Manifests from Hardcore Reality, where the Mind Thinks, the Soul is the imposer of Feeling and the Body imposes the Mind and Soul's Will while existing in Nuhfamuoh.

32.   "The Science of this Constitutional Fold - in conjunction with the Three, is solid, liquid and gas.

33.   "Mathematically measured, this aligns with the Law of number 9 in our Psychometric System. Comprehending the Circumstances of Man and the number 9, we identify the Light of Man as Intelligence.

34.   "This Intelligence that Man is, is **Pure Infinite Energy of Hardcore Reality, Corresponded with Infinitude in Vibrational Motions that range in Frequencies of G**enius, Excellence, Navigation, Consciousness and Evolution. **It is the 'Eye/I' of ISLAM.**

35.   "This Spiritual constructor of Order is an Intelligence that maintains All-Law through 5 principles of Reality. This is so, because Reality is Life, and the Natural is existence.

36. "Existence is something that the Intelligent Soul experiences for a measurement of Time in the Natural form. Reality is Pure Infinity and forever lives.

37. "And lo, the Principles of Reality are a part of the Spirit MAN and lives through the experiences of Natural Existence only when standing Square as a living perpendicular thereupon.

38. **Let MAN Comprehend the Circumstances. We as the Natural Man do not live Life because we as Spirit MAN are the Life/Hardcore Realists; and Life, lives through the Soul within the Natural Man.**

39. **"Our Principles of Reality are 5. They are: The Principle of Love, The Principle of Truth, The Principle of PEACE, the Principle of Freedom and the Principle of Justice. And these are what maintains Order in All-Law.**

40. "Executive Rulers, you must teach that the Highest level that Man can perceive is Service. Extended to another Sincerely, is the beginning to Comprehending Love.

41. "In All degree standings, Love is direct and Pure. Love varies on the table of measurements in Man's Comprehension of the Circumstances in the Consciousness of the Present Moment.

42. "There is one degree of Love that the Mother has for the Sun and the Sun has for the Mother; and there is a degree of Love that a Brother has for a neighbor and a neighbor for a Brother.

43. "There is a degree of Love a Husband has for a Wife and the Wife for the Husband; but the Greatest degree of Love is within the Reality of

the Spirit MAN. Behold, **GOD is Love to the Greatest degree. Spirit MAN is GOD in various degrees.**

44. "Through this Principle, the Equality of Man stays in the bounds of What's Right as Order persists in Man's Thinking, Feeling and Willing of All-Law.

45. "When Man Comprehends the Reality of All Circumstances in the experience of existence as his/her GOD-Consciousness, the boundless idea of color as a make up is obsolete.

46. "MAN IS GOD; GOD advances as it is degrees of Consciousness. When Man is Square in All Standings regarding this fact, the idea of being Black, Brown, Red, White, Orange, Blue, Green, Yellow or Violet is Ruled Out.

47. "There is no such thing in Nuhfamuoh as a Black Man, a White Man, or any Colored Man. MAN is GOD in Man, GOD is Love; and the God of Love is immaterial.

48. "The keys to opening the Quality of Love to every degree are: Sacrifice, Sincerity, Service, Loyalty, Honesty, Purity, Compassion, Trust and Aeal.

49. "Take these keys, open up the degrees of Love and amalgamate them into the Generator of Nuhfamuoh.

50. "Executive Rulers, you must Teach that Truth is a degree Rising Principle that never changes and never fades. Truth is Reality; Reality is ALLAH The Great I AM, Great GOD and Father of the Youniverse.

51. "Truth to the uninitiated seems to change with the Times. The ones who have yet to Be educated in Law, Thinks Truth to Be imbalanced due

to hearing Truth is One.

52.　"It confuses the unitiated to say, it is Truth that MAN is One in one instance and say it is Truth that MAN is Two and MAN is Three in the next. The Standings of the uninitiated are not Square.

53.　"For it only appears that Truth has changed to the Man out of bounds with Order. Truth Evolves with Man's Standings on the Square.

54.　"Behold this Truth. Man's National Name is Spiritual. It is I AM. Man's Natural Name is intertwined in Consciousness. It is GOD. Man's Tribal Name is Ahba, Lehunuh, Kehufa, ALI, Bazi, Rabukleh and Bumahzi. It is Structural. Man's Learned Name is Mason. It is Parental.

55.　"All of these are Truth and differ in degrees. The Order of Truth resides in Man's perception of Hardcore Reality.

56.　"Teach Man this Principle, and All-Law will manifest through Man's actions. The Perception of Reality will broaden into various degrees as Man will see Truth as One.

57.　"Executive Rulers, you must Teach that PEACE is the Harmonies MAN Thinks, Feels and Wills in the Natural Person, and through the Natural Person.

58.　"The Harmonies of MAN's Thinking, Feeling and Divine Will is Balance; and Balance is Order. The Order of Nuhfamuoh is ISLAM.

59.　**"ISLAM is Man's G**aining - **O**btaining - **D**eveloping **paradigm; It is the Youniversal Curriculum that constructs Order.**

60.　"Noble Master Builders from the Architectonic Masonic Order, has Raised up to PEACE as it is the **P**roductive – **E**ducation – **A**ctivating –

Cosmic - Energy.

61.   "I came into Nuhfamuoh as PEACE, to give to Man the variable ingredients of Equational Solution. ISLAM is the basis of All Sacred Halls of Learning in your estate. ISLAM is what I Self Law AM.

62.   "My Name as an Infinite-Divine-Dual being means PEACE, as I was sent to you by the Council of the Supreme Celestial Grand Body as the Gift of PEACE.

63.   "Intelligence-Science-Law-Architecture-and-Mathematics, are the variable ingredients that constructed this Infrastructure-Symbolism-Labor-Ancestry- and Morality of Nuhfamuoh's Governmental Rule. This Order of PEACE keeps Man stable, and Disciplined on the Square.

64.   "This Principle says **I-Self-Law-AM**, as ALLAH is the Great I AM. This PEACE spells ISLAM. The 'I' is the Intelligence of Cosmic Order. The 'S' is the Natural Person. The 'L' is the Laws of MAN'S Motions in the bounds of Light. 'A' is the Architectural structure of the Spirit MAN and the Natural man being the Evolution of the GOD in Self. It is the I AM in The Consciousness of The Present Moment. The 'M' is the Mastery of the Psychometric Mathematical Formula in All calculations of Equational Solutions.

65.   "PEACE is the Lamb come down from Cosmic Order establishing Harmony with the blood sucker. I Self - the Lamb. I AM the **L**awful - **A**rchitectural - **M**athematical - **B**asis of Nuhfamuoh.

66.   "Executive Rulers, you must Teach Freedom as the portal Gateway into the Infinite Expansions and Contractions of the Youniverse.

67.   "Within Man, there is Freedom to make decisions. There is

Freedom to live, Freedom to create, Freedom to Build Up and Freedom to tear down.

68.   "This is a 2-fold structure that this Executive Rule should utilize in enforcing All-Law. The one is terrestrial and the other is celestial.

69.   "In the terrestrial level, Freedom is established through the ism of ISLAM'S Order. There are no confines in Nuhfamuoh preventing Man from profiting in the benefits of the inheritance. The All of Man's estate is in Balance with Love, Truth and PEACE.

70.   "It is the responsibility of this Executive Rule to see to it that, Man knows the dynamics of ISLAM that constructs Freedom in Nuhfamuoh.

71.   "In the celestial level, there is Infinity-Sound-Light-Animating-Mentalism, All in Balanced Motion as the WORD.

72.   "To be Free is to Be the Traveling MAN in Spirit. MAN Travels as a Free Spirit into the -dom of Infinity-Sound-Light-Animating-Mentalism.

73.   "'Free' in the Celestial level, is Divine expression without restriction as the Light of the WORD. And the '-dom' of Freedom, is the 'Domain' of the Light of the WORD.

74.   **"Thus, Celestial Freedom is the Divine Expression of the Light of the WORD, in the Domain of Creation and Definition.**

75.   "The Elemental Domain is the canvas for the Light of the WORD'S creation. It is in this Divine Expression of Freedom that the WORD Travels as Light and manifests equilibrant form.

76.   "Equilibrant form of the WORD is GOD. And lo, GOD is the

Divine Expression in the Elemental Domain of the celestial level.

77. "In this terrestrial level here in Nuhfamuoh, the Threefold Constitution of Man Withholds the Freedom of the Celestial level. Man must know that Intelligence of Science-Law-Architecture-and Mathematics is what he/she is.

78. "It is then that Freedom can and will be Comprehended in Principle as the Gateway into the portal doors of Hardcore Reality.

79. "NO MAN can enter the portal doors to Freedom without Gaining-Obtaining- Developed Consciousness of the Masters Key.

80. "All of MAN must Travel across the unburning fiery sands in the Baheleh- yahlu Territory and up the Heyahbu-leahbuk Mountain, into the Fire of the Burning Bush that does not burn.

81. **"Teach Man that the Cultivation of I AM is a Knowledge of Self Curriculum, known as the roadmap into Freedom.**

82. "Executive Rulers, you must Teach that Justice in Principle is the Execution of what is Right. Administration of what's Right is Just. What's Right, is what's Real.

83. "There is a way that can easily seem Right to the Autonomic portion of Man that's uninitiated, which is error and out of Order. Things that are out of Order are out of Law.

84. "Justice is the sword that is used by Law Enforcement to slice at imbalanced decision making of Man, and remove all illegitimate Thinking; from Mentalism- Animating-Navigation.

85. "Your station O Executive Rule, is at the vertex of Nuhfamuoh.

Your Rule of Administration is in fact the center point and Heart of the Land. This Order of Executive Rule is the Sword, and the Administration of enforcement of Law. Enforcement of Law is the Sword's sharp edges.

86. "Everything that is Right comes from the heart of Nuhfamuoh's Order. The enforcement of Law cuts All uncalculated theory away from Man's System of decision making.

87. "The structures of ISLAMism are Arithmetically set. Formula of All Equational Phenomena Geometrically Rises and Algebraically falls back into Arithmetical setting.

88. "Hence, the bounds of Nuhfamuoh's Infrastructure-Symbolisms-and-Labors- in the-Ancestors-Morals, are calculated through the Formula of exact Order. When Man is in error, correction comes in the Formula of exact Order.

89. "Let no Man bring any means of harm to any in Nuhfamuoh. It is not Justice to cause harm or create hostility, danger, oppression or pain.

90. "Executive Rule of Order is not tyranny, or any means of Chaos. When you swing the Sword, it is only to separate Chaos from Order. The Justice of Nuhfamuoh is Order out of Chaos.

91. "Teach Man that the Sword of Justice is swung without malice, without hatred, without vengeance and without intent to harm. Every Man has within, an Executive Rule of Order. The Sword is swung from the heart to straighten out all miscalculations.

92. "On these 5 Principles does Intelligence-Science-Law-Architecture-and- Mathematics ride, as the Divine Order of Nuhfamuoh.

93. "And When the Executive Rule enforces the Law, the Principles

are the keys to the Heart. And MAN Will say: I AM Love. I AM Truth. I AM PEACE, I AM Freedom, I AM Justice.

94. "The Comprehension of the 5 Spiritual Principles is established through the 5 Points of Fellowship.

95. "As Nuhfamuoh is Built up in the 720° Geometric Stance, so it is that All initiates salute one another in a 720° stance of Geometric Order.

96. "Henceforth, when Man Masters the 5 Spiritual Principles, they are to be flagged on the Right Hand that is held High at eye level in connection with the Right Arm, as the Right Arm is on the Right Angle of the Square in 90°.

97. "The Left Arm is to stay along the side on a 180° straight angle, while the feet are on separate 45° acute angles making a 90° Square.

98. "The initiate then places the Right Hand that represents the 5 Spiritual Principles, on the Heart, and - while still standing Square says ISLAM.

99. "For the Master Builders, it is here where the 5 Points of Fellowship takes place. The Masters 5 Points of Fellowship are: Right foot to Right foot, Right knee to Right knee, chest to chest, Left hand to Back and Mouth to Ear.

100. "The Master Builders clasp the Right Hand of the other Master Mason with the Masters Grip, puts the in-step of the Right foot at the side of the other Master Builders Right in-step, lunge inward with the Right Knee to touch the other Master Mason's knee, the Chest of One Master touches the chest of the other Master, the Left Hand of one Master touches the other Master's Back - either by the shoulder, by the

neck or by the middle of the Back, to imply one's degree of Mastery to another. And the Master puts the Mouth close to the other Master's ear to Whisper the Architectonic Masonic Order of Motions.

101. "There are 3 Motions that the Masters make with the Head. First, the Mouth to Ear Motion is to the right, the second is to the left and the third is back to the right. Once this is done, the Masters take the left hand and clasps the elbow of the other to imply one degree, the left hand is either placed horizontally across the right hand clasp to imply another degree, or the left hand clasps the other Master's right shoulder to imply another degree.

102. "And these 3 Motions implies where the Master is in degree standing.

103. "Foot to foot says that we travel the course of this Journey together. Knee to knee says we are joined together from the hip.

104. "Chest to Chest says, my Order is your Order. Your Rhythm is my Rhythm in Executive Rule. Hand to back says I AM obligated to have your Back at All measurements of Time as you are to have mine.

105. "Mouth to Ear says I AM of the Silent Brotherhood from the Architectonic Masonry of Hotep; a Master Builder who will not cast the Treasures of Solomon's Treasure Chest into any measures of chaos, confusion or disharmony.

106. "The 5 Principles which are 1. Love, 2. Truth, 3. PEACE, 4. Freedom and 5. Justice, manifests equilibrant form as the WORD in a Setting of Authoritative measurements of Time.

107. "Equilibrant form of the WORD manifests God-Consciousness

in Man.

108. "Hear now All who will hear in this Executive Rule. Let this Proclamation construct Pure Infinite Order: The 5 Spiritual Principles are the Shield, Armor and Sword of Nuhfamuoh's Executive Rule. Let every Man put on the Armor and hold the Shield and Sword as a Hardcore Realist, by Generating the 5 Spiritual Principles in the Rhythm of the Heart, as the Rhythm of the Heart aligns with the cosmic Rhythm of Executive Rule and Order."

109. And Hotep sat 2 Crowns on the podium. One was Red and one was Onyx/Black.

110. Both crowns were stemmed atop, directly in the Center with a ball connected to a tassel that freely swung in a 360° circumference.

111. And Hotep said unto them: "These Crowns are for All Learned Men of Knowledge in Nuhfamuoh. We call these Crowns, **The Fez**.

112. "All Executive Rulers are to don the Black/Onyx Fez, as it represents enforcing of All-Law. You are the Master Masons who are Learned, Discerning Servants and Noble enforcers, Administering what is Right.

113. "You are Hardcore Realists, and must guard and protect the Law and the People under the Executive Order. Remember; your Station is a Service to the People of Nuhfamuoh and not the other way around.

114. "The ALI Tribe here in the Ehkeahbu Territory will also don the Black/Onyx Fez, as this clan facilitates the harmony of All-Law to other surrounding Tribes. They are the Higher Authority that Generates Order throughout Nuhfamuoh.

115.   "All Legislative and Judicial Rulers will don the Red Fez as it represents being Learned, Discerning Servants in the Order of Pure Infinity-Sound-Light- Animating-Mentalism, that manifests the Natural Order of Supreme Intelligence-of-Science-Law-Architecture-and-Mathematics.

116.   "No one is to don the Fez of any venue without first being initiated into the Order of ISLAM. For this is not a style, or fraternal custom of secrecy. This is a Crown that implies you've been through the Sacred Halls of Learning, and have been through and beyond Faluizzi.

117.   "Do not put markings on your Fez, nor tac down your tassel thereupon. The unmarked, tassel swinging Fez, represents GOD Power and Sovereignty In 360°.

118.   "When the youth of Nuhfamuoh become Learned and can Discern Order out of Chaos, it is then that they shall take the degree station of Service, stand to salute with the 720° Geometric Stance and Become a Student of the Elder Master Builders from the Guild Of Dedicated Scholars. Don their Heads with this Crown according to their station of Service.

119.   "Our Flag is a Red Flag with a Green 5 Pointed upright Star centering it. The 5 Pointed Star represents the 5 Spiritual Principles of Love, Truth, PEACE, Freedom and Justice; and the upright MAN is the Character of Comprehending All Circumstances.

120.   "Our Seal is the Circled 7 with the 4 Navigational Breaks North, East, West and South, each on the right angle of the Square in 90°.

121.   "And this 720° Geometric Stance, 5 Points of Fellowship, 5 Spiritual Principles our Fez, All Natural Law, our Flag, our Seal, Our

Tribal, National, Parental and Spiritual names and our Order of ISLAM, All represents our Cosmic, Sovereign National and Natural Government Authority Rule and Reality.

122. "We together are Hue-MAN-Being. As a collective, we are the Human Family.

123. "As I AM in the ranks of an Elder and accomplished in my Service to you All, I leave you with these qualifications to Be a Divine Nation of GODS and GODDESSES.

124. "Take these things ALLAH the Great I AM has given you and represent the Great I AM as a Divine Government of dominion that functions under the Science of I AM.

125. "And make it the Order of Proclamation: The Great I AM is what I AM, for the Masters in the Grand Government Of Dominion's Rule.

126. "Upon my departure, the Light of the Word within the Elements of Land, Fire, Water and Air will be the Light called GOD within Nuhfamuoh, under your Sovereign National Authority.

127. "It is your Birthright to Rule with GOD Authority. If you are not careful to Execute the enforcement of All-Law as All has been laid out for your prosperity, wealth and Rule, then Chaos will emerge and steal your Birthright.

128. "When I depart, do not make any statues or ornaments in my honor; for only ALLAH is Greatest and worthy of Praise and Honor.

129. "May ALLAH keep you Secure and safe in your experience of Existence in the Consciousness of the Present Moment.

130.   "Always remember: **ISLAMism is our Faith, Islamism is our Order and ISLAMism is our Creed. I AM Hotep; I Self, the** Lawful – Architectural – Mathematical - **B**asis **AM, a Hardcore Realist by Creed.**

131.   "I will come again through the Cultivation of I AM. Through your future standings you will know of my return upon one Proclaiming: I AM Hotep; **IMHOTEP** - The Supreme Gift of PEACE, Master Builder and Noble Elder known as Kebuk—The SUN of the Mother. I part on the Square with saluting you All and extending Supreme PEACE. ISLAM Executive Rule."

132.   Hotep extended his Right Hand to an eye level with his Right Arm Squared on a right angle at 90°. He then saluted the Executive Rulers in the 720° Geometric Stance, and greeted them All with the 5 Points of Fellowship.

133.   And starting from the 4th Hill, Hotep traveled East and went into the ALI Temple/Lodge to extend his greetings and final Orders.

134.   From the ALI Temple/Lodge, he traveled into the 3rd Hill into the AL Temple/Lodge to extend his greetings and final Orders. From the AL Temple/Lodge he traveled into the West and Navigated North into the 5th Hill at the Moor Temple/Lodge to extend his greetings and final Orders.

135.   From the Moor Temple/Lodge, he traveled East and Navigated South into the 2nd Hill at the Temple of Dey to extend his Greetings and final Orders. From the Temple/Lodge of Dey, he traveled into the West and Navigated North into the 6th Hill at the Bey Temple/Lodge to extend his greetings and final Orders.

136. From the Bey Temple/Lodge he traveled East and Navigated South into the 1ˢᵗ Hill at the El©™Temple/Lodge to extend his greetings and Final Orders. From the El©™Temple/Lodge he traveled West and Navigated North into the 7ᵗʰ Hill at the ALLAH Temple/Lodge.

137. And from there, Hotep went up into the Heyahbu-leahbuk Mountain to the Burning Bush that didn't burn. He said to the unburning Bush of Fire: "It is finished. The variable to the Equational Solution of the Council of GODS has Built Up Nuhfamuoh.

138. "May ALLAH the Great I AM Be pleased. For the Lamb of Nuhfamuoh has given the eternal Seeds of Hardcore Reality to the Master Builders; and they shall Cultivate the soil of Nuhfamuoh, for I AM to manifest as the Birthright of the People.

139. "It's the Morning! I can see the Future; and I shall return as IMHOTEP - The Hardcore Realist by Creed! As for the Present Moment, I AM returning to my Pure Infinite Throne." **Hotep entered the Fire of the Burning Bush that didn't Burn and was never seen again in Nuhfamuoh.**

140. He came upon the Youniversal Ladder and climbed up to the 4th Stair where Solomon's Throne resided. He saluted Solomon; and Solomon stood from his Throne, and pressed Hotep's hand with the Masters Grip. They greeted one another on the 5 Points of Fellowship, and Hotep departed.

141.   He climbed up into the Abode of ALLAH the Great I AM to sit in his Throne beneath THE ALLi and he shined thereupon as the Hardcore Realist.

⇐   O — O — O — O — O   ⇒

THE FINAL THOUGHT

After carefully reviewing and analyzing this Book of Hardcore Reality, I hope that it done its portion of service to you. The Spark should Be manifest that either furthers your Journey Traveled in the quest for Self Knowledge, or shows you a course of Beginning to seek within, to Learn and Discern your station of Service in this World.

We're all here for a Purpose. At a particular measurement in History, we better Comprehended such Circumstances due to our Characters being more Balanced in facts rather than technology, gadgets, games and fictions. Comprehending your Reality as Pure Infinite Energy/PIE/PI rather than seeing your Reality as the material World, gives you the advantage over those who are in the dark to order. As PI, there comes a Balance in degree standings of Comprehending the Consciousness of your vision enveloped in the Infinite Expansions of All-Law. Thinking is an unlimited Freedom representing Order; being Raised up into the Thinking of Service represents Gaining-Obtaining-Developing Consciousness/God Consciousness. For there's no Greater degree than Service. Contributing a God-Conscious Creation into a profane world is All of our Purpose and responsibility.

Our differences reside in our perceptual Comprehensions of the Set Circumstances.

What I mean by that is our mere Temperaments and how we retain data one phase into another, are not the same. Some are Choleric and of a Fire Element - as am I. Some are Melancholic and of a Land Element. Some are Phlegmatic and of a Water Element, and some are Sanguine and of an Air Element. This says that some Characters, are of contractive tendencies while others, are of expansive tendencies (in other words, some are introverted, others extroverted.) Some may see our differences of Character and assume hopelessness in Oneness, while others may see the benefits of every Character having Individual Creative Quality (BHR 6:52-56). We cannot all Be on the same level at the same time.

However, we can All work together with our Individual Creative Qualities, to maintain Order in our Purpose and dealings. Upon learning that we are to Raise up into a God-Consciousness that serves the world with our contributions thereof, we take our differences and put them in order. Building something is not done alone with one tool. There are various tools in the shed that has an order. This is the order we are to learn.

As of Right now, we've shown a lack of Comprehension in this era and measurement of Time. The material world and material gain, is the outlook of many. This is a current representation of chaos. Thinking with no bounds disrupts structure. Our current thoughts, are the blind creative force, constructing materialism into manifest, as the dominant desire and necessity in society. Conscious of Order or not, many today are making contributions of the like into the world without consideration of Reality. Boundless Thinking, is what constructs Characters of Greed, lust, envy, hatred, rage, and Selfishness. And from these Characteristics, there's found overpopulated prisons, reigns of Rule by Corporate government, Unjust courts and politics, slavery, poverty, gangs, savagery, promiscuity, disease, fun and play, concealed history and facts, racism and so much more chaotic lunacy making a profane world. In such uninitiated Thinking of chaos, ones are more concerned about a "profit" coming to save them from this contribution of destruction, coming from "The God" of this profane world—

The **Corporate** **G**overnment-**O**rdinance-**D**epartments, rather than seeking to learn that All Salvation comes from within. The God of this profane world and its "legal tender" (Federal Reserve Notes), are only fictions and material manifestations that exist on paper. The God of this profane world and its profit; are just boundless Thoughts of Chaos. It's not good, nor is it evil. For the uninitiated, there's a lack of Comprehending the Purpose of its manifestation. As a consequence, greed emerges as a Characteristic, with the idea that success surrounds mass accumulations of the profit. Once it becomes a facilitating theory, one gets lost in the false perception of power and becomes egotistical, shrewd, and careless about Reality. This is the current condition of our mental status.

It's the season for hearing; those who have an ear to hear, Comprehend the measurement of Reality.

The Focus of this Work is to contribute a Hardcore Realist Education to the People. Such a Curriculum starts with Self. Think...if the Corporate Government, Merchants/Banks, and all commercial material/legal tender/Federal Reserve Notes lost its power today, who, what and where would you be tomorrow without it? You are what you Think; who, what, where are you; when, why and how are you? If you've never contemplated this on your own, then you've been mentally consumed by the fiction - you're living in OZ under the mental spell of a fictional power, facilitated by a fictional Wizard. An education of a Hardcore Realist deals in **I**ntelligence-**S**cience-**L**aw-**A**rchitectural-**M**athematical-**I**nstructional- **S**ublime-**M**entalism. Knowing that we are a part and portion of the Elements Land-Water-Air-Fire, begins the course of Study we'd have to undergo. These Elements are the "Four-Parents" of our existence in the Natural. They function together to contribute to Humanity the quality of existence. Human Beings are walking, living, breathing examples of the Laws of the Youniverse and Elements. We are in fact a part of the Elements, and the Elements are our "Four-Parents" – A part of our Natural Order. If these Elements function in an accord together by All-Law, then we as Humanity must Learn to Discern those Laws, that we may Serve—as do the Elements with Conscious contribution towards the uplifting of Humanity's cause. When the lessons are printed for this Book of Hardcore Reality (BHR), we will begin to unveil this Knowledge of Self Curriculum, course for course, degree for degree.

We want to Be clear on our standings regarding this structure of ISLAM. As presented in this Book of Hardcore Reality, ISLAM is not religion or a part of any religious custom, practice or tradition. ISLAM is Education, and only spells in acronym, the subject matters through which we will travel in various degrees (BHR 6:89-90). This is Order and of Ancient construction. We want to be clear on our standings regarding this structure of ISLAM, and Freemasonry also. This Book of Hardcore Reality in no way, shape or form, represents Freemasonry. The Build of Freemasonry is of modern design, of secrecy and oath, and represents fraternal clubism. This design of ISLAM and Masonry—representing the construction of this Curriculum is of Ancient, Operative Structure. We're not speculating anything, nor do we intend to keep Secret the Sacred Jewels of Solomon. The Operative Guild of Master Builders to which we refer, is an inner Reality of Law. As you will learn from us, Akh-Hulebuk represents the Family of cells within you, following the "Blueprint of Law" drawn up by the Infallible Architect of Mentalism, to build up Nuhfamuoh - which represents your BODY. Your BODY IS your shelter. Thus, this Masonry of Ancient and the ISLAM ascribed to it, is Operative, is Sacred and the Knowledge of Self Curriculum designed to uplift those who are feeling abandoned, left out, feeling as though they don't fit or belong in any religions, and who want to know the Truth.

Our aim is to serve the People with their Ancient

Order in a Modern form that they can Comprehend. We are in the Works of manufacturing a Modern Day Mystery School. To be clear, this is our standings. The "Mother" in this Order is no "Widow". Hiram Abiff - The Master Builder, was Raised/Cultivated from the shallow grave -via- the Masters Grip of Solomon, and lives today.

In this Know Thyself Curriculum again, a Mason is a Crafts-Man/Molecular- Autonomical-Nucleus, Building up Nuhfamuoh/ Nuh=Body, Fa=Order, Mu=Degrees, Oh=Land, Water, Fire, Air. We want to make sure that this is clear and comprehended by Freemasons and Al-ISLAM fanatics, or by any who just enjoy having an opposing approach to conversation. **I AM strongly against debating, arguing, competition and/or fighting with words due to disagreeable Characters.** The objective is to uplift the People, not provide them with front row seats to an unnecessary fight. We are not against any structure, nor do we look to argue, debate or fight with disagreeable Characters. This degree of Learning, Discerning and Serving is Order and not Chaos. There has been enough foolishness, ignorance, selfishness and division among us. We're Solutionists! This composition of ISLAM presented is PEACE; Peace for us is the **P**roductive-**E**ducation-**A**ctivating-**C**osmic-**E**nergy **in yours and my Youniversal Consciousness.** We are for PEACE and not destruction. So if you have been inspired in any way by this body of work, don't allow any to convince you that this is something that it is not. This is not Freemasonry, Al-ISLAM, religion, or fraud. This is yours and my Educational venture.

As an Author, Student, Teacher, Brother and Hardcore Realist, I've experienced some of the most disturbing conflict a Human Being can register. I've been called sensitive; I've been told that I take things too personal. I've been outcast and ostracized by so-called fellow Brothers.

I've been told that I'm hot headed and clingy, too strict, too serious, push too hard and so much more. Within the various incidents that occurred among so-called fellow People of Righteousness and myself, what became unmasked to me was how an anti-social, psychopathic and two-faced people can be pretend righteous and complacent in their climb. In trying to Become a part of the circles, I've been pushed away for attempting to encourage moving out of complacency by Way of intense study, discipline and serving those that needed help. There was so much arguing, debating and justifying not growing, that I—as a Choleric Temperament had to discipline myself to Become a passive-aggressive persona and shut down on Brothers. When I did, the arguing stopped, the debating stopped; but the complacency and pretend Righteousness didn't. I had to learn that, People in the dark cannot see the Way. When they are set on practicing something a certain way, nothing is going to pull them from that complacent comfort zone. They will fight, debate, argue, and maintain a disagreeable Character to guard their perception of a text, ayat, verse, chapter, or something a leader of old said. My experience taught me that things will not change for the better while, involved with people holding to the things of old that have got us as a collective, nowhere. Such a thing is not Brotherhood, Sisterhood, or anything constructive to the cause of upliftment. It's not the things of old or the leaders of old that I've had a bad experience with, it's the psychopathic, complacent, two-faced, argumentative, debating selfish people.

Fact of the matter is, it is because of my Christian upbringing, and support from my Christian family that I've made it this far. It is because of my learning everything Malcolm X taught that I've made it this far. It is because of my wanting to be like Minister Malcolm X, that I learned about The Supreme Wisdom Lessons of the Nation of ISLAM. It was because of the Supreme Wisdom Lessons, that I learned about the 5%

Nation of Gods and Earths, and studied the Knowledge-Wisdom-Cipher and plus degree to gain Zig-Zag-Zig of the Structure, and have a zeal to want to work for and with the 85. It is because of my Journey in the 5% Cipher, that I learned about Moorish Science, Noble Drew Ali, Nationality and Principle, and studied the Moorish Holy Koran and the Holy Instruments from the Prophet. It is because of my current stand as a Moorish Scientist, that I learned the Mystery Systems structures and seen the Science of Ancient Operative Masonry, became an Anthroposophist and studier of all disciplines. My journey consists of Christianity, ISLAM, 5%, Malcolm X Teachings and speeches, the Moorish Science Temple of America, Anthroposophy, Kemetic Science and All Parham Philosophy of Minister Anna Parham, Frederick "Skeet' Parham and Gardenia Parham. My Journey through these Chambers proved that there is nothing wrong with them. All of the disciplines are good, and good for the individual. It is the people (some of them) involved in the disciplines, making them dogmatic rather than Spiritual, religious rather than Real.

One of the main reasons I've constructed this Book, is to eliminate the unnecessary arguing and debating done amongst Brothers and Sisters regarding the Order of things that have already been done. This is for those who want to Evolve, and for those who feel pushed away by psychological, sociopathical tyrants that like to argue, debate and fight with those spiritual disciplines. As I have said, the things done before this Book of Hardcore Reality are excellent Orders. The problems emerge from the lack of unveiling Lessons to the People, that will decode the Sacred Works, and eliminate unnecessary argument, the lack of qualified teachers who themselves Comprehend the Sacred Works and refuse to argue and debate, and the lack of them knowing how to conjoin what is considered Science and religion. With these ingredients missing from the legitimate Orders of Spiritual discipline, there's a chaotic social setting due to a lack of opened Sacred Halls of Learning. Unnecessarily, our People combat over the differences of uninitiated perception, and destroy the opportunities to unite Thoughts, and Build off of one another. Uninitiated perception causes this unnecessary separation that discourages the seeker away from the settings, because they represent Chaos from where the Seeker stands. Any that have been initiated into any Chambers of Spiritual Discipline, know that argument, debate and combat are unnecessary and represents insecurity, folly and confusion. The Book of Hardcore Reality eliminates this Family Feud. By this not being "new time religion", all Brothers and Sisters - Christian, Muslim, Hebrew, Moorish Moslems, 5%ers, NOI, Kemetic Scientist, Anthroposophist, etc. can participate in building from this curriculum. The intended design, is for All to get on one accord with intentions of guarding our youth from the folly we've created. We Learn, and then give to them the Productive-Education-Activating-Cosmic-Energy that we've collectively lacked for many eras now, and show them how to function in a fiction world of Chaos with Order, an Intelligent tone, and confidence that suppresses ignorance, argument, debate and combat.

Think ... are we really retaining what we should as uninitiated participants of spiritual disciplines that are watered down by dogmatic religious practice today? Here's how to find out. Every religious order of spiritual discipline has within their paradigms, how to construct Heaven on Earth, or the Hereafter, or Paradise, or Culture/Freedom or some form of salvation. Whatever your religion details have you learned how to:

1. Follow the Stars, and listen to the Earth explain her delicacies?

2. Have you been taught about corporate, artificial status, and how to come from under this denationalized state into the Sovereign National in the Natural Person?

3.   Do you know how to survive if a National disaster emerged?

4.   Can you Build a Youniversal Safe Haven from harm?

5.   Can you mix chemicals and clean water in case the water supply goes bad, or make clean water from thin air?

6.   Can you plant and grow food?

7.   Can you say you are a Nation outside of corporate fiction, and be recognized in the World Court as a Nation?

8.   Are you an Artificial Person, or a Human Being to the Corporate state that is incorporated into the Corporate Federal Government?

9.   Why/Why not?

10. Is African American, Black, Negroe, Nigga, Colored Folk, B#?°*, Thug, Stone, Vice Lord, Folks, Soul, Disciple and Gangster considered being Human Being, or Artificial criminal persons?

11. Is inmate, convict, detainee, resident, criminal, slave, bondsman and prisoner considered being Human beings, or artificial savage expendable stock, chattel property and persons?

12. Are you connected to the cosmic expansions?

13. How/How not?

14. Who and What are you?

15. What does your religion of today teach you about these things?

Take this little quiz and research to find out the Truth and facts. You may be surprised at/by what you come across.

I'm sure, that some can easily answer these questions while others may struggle. No hard time should be given to any who may not have been taught these important components to building Heaven on Earth, Paradise, the Hereafter, etc. This is where we've oftentimes gone wrong as the uninitiated religious fanatics.

Never ridicule a Brother or Sister for a religious affiliation preference.

Again, it is not the religious order that is bad, wrong or imbalanced. It is the fact that the Real Science of it all has been removed, or is being held back from the People; leaving them to Be Building uninitiated perceptions that they argue and debate with against other Brothers and Sisters. Anytime any Brother or Sister joins a religious order, commend them, congratulate them, and support them, because they've made a choice to do what is right. Don't contend with them, ridicule them, challenge them, or try making them think that they've done something wrong. For how can we make one wrong for wanting what's right? We are to Build one another up in all instances, not debate the differences in uninitiated perception. All can't and won't see things the same way all of the time. Perception is Thinking, and retaining degree Comprehension of Hardcore Reality (BHR 5:35). To argue or debate ISLAM is absurd. Uninitiated perception creates opinionated viewpoints and standoffish characters. This is why the Book of Hardcore Reality is not religious. Comprehension of Circumstances of Reality comes from a Balanced Character. A Balanced Character represents Order.

The Lessons to follow are the Modern Day Sacred Halls that will unveil the Secrets, the connection to spirit and Science, and the Order of a Hardcore Realist. By the time you're done in the Student degree of lessons, you'll be putting the corporate government on notice about your

Freedom from their jurisdiction. You'll know your Body, you'll Be familiar with your cosmic connections, Nature and her Laws and so much more. I know that you may not be used to any willingly giving you the answers. Well, I'm not afraid of the backlash. I'm not under the control of any new time religious dogma, and I'm a Hardcore Realist. As a Sheik in the Moorish Science Temple, it is my responsibility to uplift, and imitate Noble Drew Ali.

"Imitate - to model oneself after the behavior or actions (of another)."

When you research and find out the actions and behavior of this Prophet, you'll find that he labored to serve the People of that era with a Mystery System, Sacred Halls, Principles, Keys to Freedom and their National Name.

He done so much more than what I'm expressing, that I can't name it all. I'd have to write a book just about his accomplishments in Service to the People.

Many perceive imitating Noble Drew Ali as parroting his sayings, and/or his writings. My perception of imitating Noble Drew Ali, surrounds serving Humanity with Hardcore Reality. Moorish Science is my faith. Moorish American is my Nationality. This may not be something you're interested in, or know anything about. I shouldn't try to force my faith on you, so I don't. I gave you the Book of Hardcore Reality as my portion of Comprehension. If you're wondering why I didn't inform you until now that I'm a Moorish American, it is because I didn't want you to pre-judge me or stigmatize the work. Some Moors may not agree with what I've done here. I'm okay with that, because I've done what I'm supposed to do. If you'd so happen to be interested in a Moorish Science Temple, contact me and I'll help you with that. Also, I kept that part away from the work, because this work is about you and not about me.

149

I'm not trying to convert you into anything. I just want to serve you with my perception of Self Knowledge, that may help you to better Comprehend what your choice faith is - Be it Christianity, ISLAM, Al-ISLAM, Hebrew, Moorish Science, Kemetic Science, etc.

So that's it. I hope that you will support us on this journey as we work to serve and support you. In conclusion, I see no better way to close this out, other than with the Words of my main Teacher, Mentor and Uncle. Thank you all for reading this work; and may your journey have balance.

"There's nothing more important than learning what your Purpose in this world is, Dre. Do that, and make your contribution to society. Don't be afraid of those that may try keeping you down, and don't back down from their roar.

Never worry about anything that you can't control, because it causes unnecessary stress. Make sure that you learn love, and love yourself. I'm a Hardcore Realist nephew, and I'm only going to teach you what's Real; you dig?"

Frederick "Skeet" Parham

The God Degrees

A Sample Lesson Booklet of Light

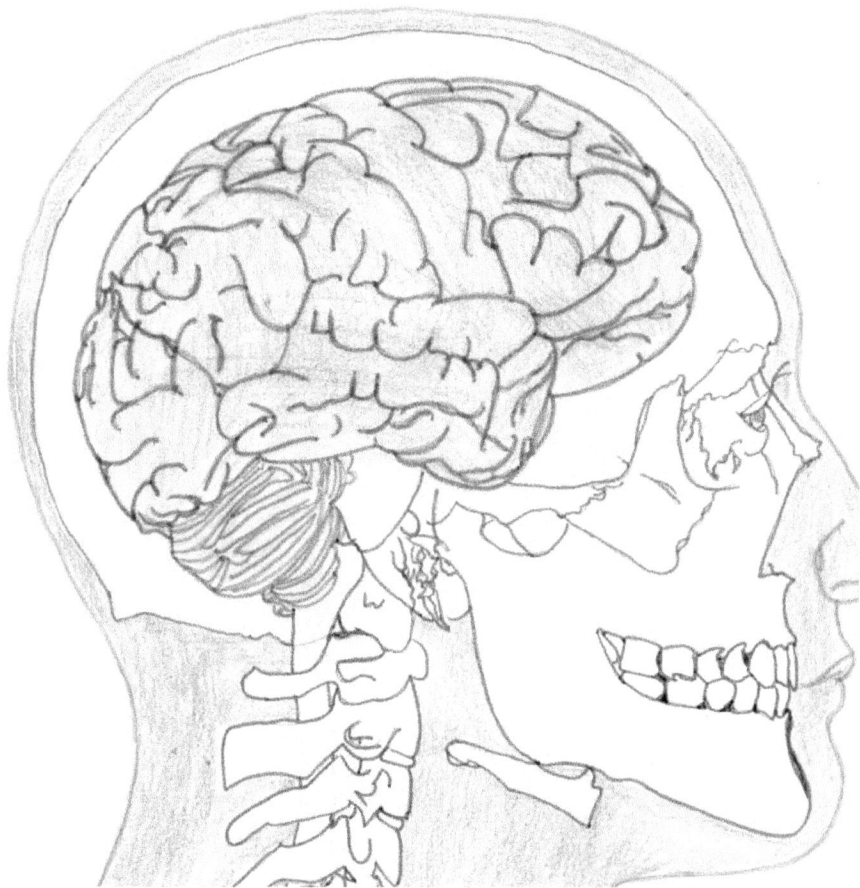

By Sheik Andrell Parham Bey©™

AN INTRODUCTION INTO THE SAMPLE LESSONS

Let's be clear about a few things before going off into our sample lessons. Regarding "Learning," - it is a specific discipline branching out into many layers and levels. It should be obvious that this discipline - in this era and time Measurement, has been removed from the venues of most academic educational fields. It has been analyzed and discussed amongst many who have experienced, and had close up encounters in/with, the current educational academic platform to which the conclusion was reached, that such an extended venue is counter-productive. Some passed, some failed and some dropped out of this venue.

One thing that all parties of the discussion agreed upon, was how this counterproductive venue of academic education only offers drills of committing data to memory.

The Cultivation of I AM is in no way tied into/with the Public School academic field and venue. This small Book of Hardcore Reality, is a Youniversal Curriculum that provides an Education in Self Knowledge and Self Government, and all surrounding subject matters in relation thereto. The Book of Hardcore Reality does not deal in any racial discriminations or any psycho-socio perceptions of ignorance, foolishness or stupidity (BHR 9:45-47). There is only one race in this World, and this is called 'The Human Race'. There is no age limitation connected to this structure of education. It is everyone's job to learn how to deal in Reality and Teach our Children to Rise accordingly. At this degree, we will then be qualified to serve Humanity with the Principles of

Love, Truth, PEACE, Freedom and Justice.

At this point in time measurement, we know that our youth are not developing into mature Human Beings, equipped to deal in Reality. Conscious contributions are not being made and/or extended to them. We can't blame Public Schools for being what they are, because we shouldn't depend on any Public School curriculum to educate our children. Public School curriculums are only multicultural bases that offer skills dealing in functioning in an artificial corporate world of commerce. Their responsibility does not deal in developing a sense of Consciousness with a mind and body connection, or in getting a Student to learn who they are in Reality. Such a responsibility is ours as Parents, Uncles, Aunties, Grandmother/Fathers and Cousins. According to this descriptive detail, Public Schools then are not: under developing our children.

We are in fact under developing our children by not serving them with a curriculum dealing in Reality.

"Curriculum - all the courses of study offered by an educational institution. A course of study, often in a specialized field."

"Education - knowledge or skill obtained or developed by learning - the act or process of education or being educated - the field of study concerned with teaching and learning pedagogy."

"Lesson: class - an assignment or exercise in which something is being learned."

"Learn - to gain knowledge, comprehension or mastery of, through study or experience - to acquire through experience."

Webster's II New College Dictionary

Looking upon the meanings of these terms, we find that a curriculum withholds the courses of study offered by an educational institution - often in a specialized field. Are we as Elders being responsible by offering our youth courses of study in the specialized field of Reality? Are we in the homes, being the educational institutional teachers of Temperament, perception, facts, current and ancient events, the necessities of Formula in Mathematics and the practice of Comprehending Formula - via- the exercising of moving numbers by calculation in equational form; Physiology, health, time, work, hygiene, commerce, mercantile law, being Nationalized or denationalized, the differences between a corporation called the UNITED STATES and a Sovereign Republic called the Continental United States of Al-Morocco/America, Human Rights, indigenous rights, Bill of Rights, Treaty Laws, Natural Persons, Artificial persons, statutory codes, Natural Law, how to deal in the Present Moment as a Conscious Reality, ignorance, violence, entertainment, Public School, what to do in it, why, etc, etc.?

A collective change starts with being able to deal in, accept and look into the Reality of our Circumstances. If we have not constructed courses of study in these few mentioned fields as educational institutional teachers of what's Real, what's not Real and how to stand on what's Real, then we have failed our children, not the Public School System. It is our responsibility to educate our youth in these areas, before allowing them anywhere near a Public School academic educational curriculum. In this way, we have supplied their outlook on existence with Reality, and the Comprehension of what they are dealing with. As Mother Evolution Raises them up, no commercial advertising, no subliminal messages of entrapment, no esteem issues or peer pressures would knock them off Balance or focus as a Supreme Consciousness that is developing the adept Mastery of the Present Moment.

An active and effective education that comes from the Home is the teaching of Skills and learning the Knowledge thereof. We know that our youth today lack social skills, and thinking skills outside of memorization. Outside of being combative or argumentative, they lack application skills - where Formula,

Natures Law, current events that affect future standings and many educational platforms, are not connected in/with their Thinking Systems; and they lack the Comprehension of taking application projects and making them Building Blocks of Character.

Learning Skills are lacking majorly. We have not educated our youth about learning. To learn is to gain Knowledge, and skills by studying something, experiencing something, or being taught something by another. Resultingly, one will acquire the particular ability to do what is learned! All bad habits are learned; they do not come Natural to anyone. As we are seeing, entertainment, entertainers, the streets, Public Schools, bad habits, gangs and all corporate structures, have been the leading teachers of all surrounding disorder. This is our time to change this Chaos with bringing Order out of it.

The Cultivation of I AM is the Curriculum designed to reconstruct the specialized field of Reality necessary to establish order in society. The curriculum is not the Lessons. As the Director of Education, and Author of this Educational venture in the Fall Back Movement, I AM still building with potential writers and Teachers, that they may willingly contribute their portions of Comprehensions of the Book of Hardcore Reality through lessons. The willing at this point are small in number. Hence, a lot of brainstorming and collective perception building is currently underway, breaking the curriculum down step-by-step for collective lesson writing. What both Neal Bey and I have constructively agreed on - as we both want to contribute through this Fall Back

Movement's educational structures of development for our youth in society, was for me to set the bar with a sample lesson booklet connected to the back of this curriculum.

Know that your participation and supporting purchase of this curriculum contributes to this educational cause of taking responsibility for what goes on in our youth's heads. We're keeping the price as low as possible, because this is not about the author making money. This is about all of us coming together to shut down our own means to fail, and rise up in order. If we had it where we didn't have to ask for any financial support, then we wouldn't. We need the financial support to continue publishing the forthcoming works for our future development. If you'd like to contact me, my information will be made available in the end of this sample lesson booklet. My Teachers and Mentors—Minister Anna Parham, Frederick "Skeet" Parham, Gardenia Parham, Kevin Mcletchie El-G.S.D.M., Mary Palmer, the Moors Order of the Round Table, Labron Neal Bey©™-G.S.D.M. , Mary M. of Criminon and experience itself, along with my Brothers on the Square, Sheik Jeffery Carmichael Bey©™, Sheik Jason Taylor El©™, Sheik Reginald Kelly El©™, Alfred Moore Bey©™, Tommy Smith El©™, Sheik William Riley El©™, Andre Patterson and Sheik Rickey Robinson El©™, to you all, I extend Supreme Love, Honor, Thanks and Respect, for helping me reach the Height at which I stand Square. I hope that you all can appreciate and see your portions of working with me through this work.

To all Students, may this new beginning be beneficial to the cause of our getting a Real Education, that will re-establish balance in our existence and Comprehension of our affairs. Let's FALL BACK from fiction and Raise Up in Reality Squarely.

Director of Education

Fall Back Movement

Squarely Standing,

PSYCHOMETRIC MATHEMATICS

Mathematics is an exact structure of Science, dealing in All Motions spawning from sound/vibration in every manifest frequency of positive and negative fields of Energy in the Youniverse. This discipline and structure of Science gives Hardcore Reality its pulsation. The Rhythmic Motions of ebb and flow in the Youniverse translates into the Consciousness of the Present Moment, giving every Individual the ability to calculate Inner visions of Vibration into perception. Perception itself is a Mathematical quality innately connected to Consciousness, automatically creating Psycho-spiritual Formula, to Socially and emotionally define every step in developing calculations of Character.

This is Mathematics. It is in fact, an area of Mathematics most of us were never introduced to in our Educational journey.

Thought is visual situations and Circumstances of perception, Formulating ideal Solutions and conclusions in our existence. What we perceive through our Consciousness of the Present Moment, Mathematically becomes the basis for Formulating Character that Comprehends surrounding perceptual Circumstances (BHR 5:35). Every Individual perception can range from negative fields into positive fields, and positive fields into negative fields. What happens is, things at that point can become mixed up amongst individuals, and contradiction will seem to be ideal conclusions. Remember that Mathematics is an exact Science of discipline. The basis of Thinking is Mathematical Formula. Thought manifests as an innate mechanical force, projecting through systems - both Spiritual and Natural. Systematic Thinking, formulates structured production in our intentions and development. As children, for example, we're then able to perceive data as it is exhibited through display, or conveyed, and formulate the idea of locomotion. The process of such a mathematical calculation is innate. We in fact formulated as small children: Walking equals balance over Focus times Motion - W=B/F(M). In this Math, the makeup of our Character calculates all Systematic Structures that gives the laboring ability to crawl, grab onto things and utilize them to stand up. Are you following the theory?

As things advanced, Formulas were written down. Numbers are only attributed elements used to exercise calculating Formulated Thought, or Systematic Thinking. This is an ancient concept. Such an ancient precision of Mathematical practice has been kept from what is considered a layman today. This era of Mathematical theory, deals more in juggling numbers rather than systems that construct Formula for Character, that Comprehends all Circumstances. Numbers at this height are only symbols that represents Thinking processes. I'm introducing the Ancient Mathematics dealing in this Systematic Thinking. Those before me who made public the same systematic form of Mathematical Thinking were C.M. Bey©™, the Honorable Elijah Muhammad, and Clarence 13X"ALLAH". I honor and look up to these Teachers, but I don't want to present anything that has already been mathematically established by them, because it would open the door for unnecessary argument, debate and confusion by uninitiated Students of those disciplines. So, I've allowed this ancient structure of Thinking to pull out of my perceptual Consciousness, a recreation I call **Psychometric Mathematics**. Through this Mathematical paradigm, numbers are connected to Thoughts, in systems of measurements that constructs Formulas, causing particular calculations that gives particular solutions and conclusions. I don't have high expectation for the Psychometric Mathematics being broadly embraced or respected by worldly mathematicians of current era practice.

160

This systematic structure of calculating -via- Formulated Thinking, will probably be a paradoxical theory to them. This Scientific Discipline, is not for them, nor is it any challenge to their adept standards of mathematical ability. This Scientific Discipline, is for those of us who are not afraid of learning how to translate mathematical calculation into the activity of our production. This is done by Comprehending Formula.

"Psychometric Mathematics - Systematic Thinking arranged in degree Formulas, unveiling how to combine laws of Intelligence and channels of perception into psychologized calculations of activity of Reality, by/with/through exact measurements of numbers, signs, symbols, psycho-spiritual variables and all calculated associations and relationships with the Mystic chambers of psychology. The physiology of the Human anatomy, astrology, sociology and Nature."

My intentions are to establish a fresh concept that ranges in degrees, that all may learn various ways to utilize this arrangement as a means to Think Systematically; with psychological mathematical mentalism. I've organized terminology with numerical value that both represent a perceptual order of Systems, that manifests according to the set up of the numerical formation. As there are 3 degrees in this educational venue, there are 3 Formulas constructed for the 3 degrees of initiates to build from. The Formulas I have constructed are only mere products of my perception of Reality. As one advances in standing, there should come the ability to arrange your own Formula and show that Einstein was not the 1st or last great Mathematician to construct Formulas of Scientific Discipline. **We are All in Spirit, Traveling Sounds Animating the Light of Consciousness into the Present Moment. The expression of this Infinite Consciousness is rising degrees of GOD (BHR 9:75-76). We are All in Reality, GODS experiencing existence in an Authoritative Rule of Time measurements through the Womb- of-**

MAN's Evolution (Nuhfamuoh the Natural Mother). Hence we are very capable of establishing Mathematical Formula like no other, that can and will reconstruct Order back into our existence today. That is what this Psychometric Mathematical table represents.

Systematically, the Math Table is set up according to All-Laws of the Youniverse. This first degree Formula, consists of Arithmetical Rules of calculating numbers (addition, subtraction, multiplication, division, fractions, decimals, percents, etc.) with psychologizing systems ascribed to them. For this **Student who Learns the Way**, a small definition will be given with each term, that a beginner's guide may be utilized in working the Math. This Mathematical structure belongs to you as it does me, and all who intend on utilizing it to construct Order in our existence, to in turn save our youth with Divine Sacrificial Service.

You will see the Alphabet of Akh-Hulebuk connected to this table while not connected to the Student's Formula. The Alphabet of Akh-Hulebuk is utilized in this Student degree when an individual concept is being broken down, not calculated in the Psychologizing structure of Building. Outside of this sample form, all will be explained and exhibited before we go into our Math Tables.

We will first re-familiarize our Thinking Systems with Youniversal Law/Principle.

YOUNIVERSAL LAW/PRINCIPLE

1. The Principle of Mentalism - "The ALL is MIND; the Universe is Mental."

2. The Principle of Correspondence - "As above, so below; as below, so above. As within, so without, as without, so within."

3. The Principle of Vibration - "Nothing rests; everything moves; everything vibrates."

4. The Principle of Polarity - "Everything is Dual; everything has poles; everything has its pair of opposites like and unlike are the same; opposites are identical in nature, but different in degree; extremes meet; all truths are but half-truths; all paradoxes may be reconciled."

5. The Principle of Rhythm - "Everything flows out and in; everything has its tides; all things rise and fall; the pendulum's swing to the right is the measure of its swing to the left; rhythm compensates."

6. The Principle of Cause and Effect - "Every cause has its effect, every effect has its cause; everything happens according to Law; change is but a name for Law not recognized; there are many planes of causation, but nothing escapes the Law."

7. The Principle of Gender - "Gender is in everything; everything has its Masculine and Feminine Principles; Gender manifests on all planes."

> "The Principles of truth are seven; he who knows these understandingly possesses the Magic Key before whose

touch all the doors of the temple fly open."

The Kybalion

It was imperative to give these Youniversal Principles of Law to any Student who may have been unaware. When we review these 7 Articles of Order, we are looking at Systematic Thinking. Before these 7 Principle Articles Formulates a Masters Key, they are first seen as 7 different individual concepts that must be first Comprehended separately. Once they are separately Comprehended as separate systems within our very own Youniverse of Mentalism, then they can start to be calculated to structure singular conclusions of manifestation. This is how I want you to deal in the Psychometric Mathematics. Each concept must first be Comprehended separately. Once they are Comprehended as singular systems, they can then be calculated to manifest singular conclusions of solution. All Students must learn this along with Universal Principles, before utilizing it to unveil the Students Mathematical direction along the Way in this Know Thyself curriculum. Let's learn the math, and its opposite table in systems:

PSYCHOMETRIC MATH TABLE

0_1 The Macrocosmic ALL, or PI = ⌐ = 360, or 3.14, 22/7

1.   The WORD = ϵ = 1,088

2.   The Light, or Order = ⌐ =186,000, or 3.360

3.   Motion/Travel = ⅄ = 34^{10}

4.   Elements/square = ⌐ =90

5.   Time/Space = ⌣ =60

6.   Equilibrant form = ⊥ = 7/360

7.   GOD-Consciousness = ↑ = 90/360 ÷ 7/360 = 12 6/7

8.   Creation/Definition = ⌒ = 9

9.   Natural Person = Ω = 1+11.2

0_2 Microcosm of Macrocosm = ⟋ = 720, $8 = \frac{360}{360}$ = ALLAH

THE OPPOSITE TABLE

0_1 Of All Abyss

1. Illusion
2. Darkness or Chaos
3. Stillness
4. Unmeasured Standing
5. Uncalculated
6. Malformit
7. Unconscious instincts
8. Destruction
9. Artificial Person

0_2 Corporation/dismal crypt

When we learn the fundamental concepts of the terms and how they relate to us and Youniversal Law, we can start out with calculating the concepts with addition. Before going into a Formula, the Student should go through the Math table and learn the data of each term. All Students should then calculate the information and learn to explain the sum solution it all gives in its exact arrangement. When a valid Comprehension is reached, the Student should carefully go through the Book of Hardcore Reality, and begin calculating the equations as they are found in the verses in this manner to become sharp at explaining the meanings to concepts. An example would be:

I AM, a Natural Person.

Before anything can be calculated, the Student must ponder over the equational statement of addition. What does this mean; to be a Natural Person? First, we'd want to go to a dictionary and see what we can find.

"Natural - produced by Nature and free from artificiality."

"Person - the composite of characteristics that make up an individual personality."

"Natural Person - the composite of characteristics making up the individual persona produced by Nature and is free from artificiality."

This is the Natural Person. Hence, **I AM the composite of Nature's elements within an Individual Consciousness, free from artificiality**. This alludes to having a specific temperament that connects to an element that defines the content of my Character. This is the beginning to Comprehending the singular system. The Alphabet of Akh-Hulebuk is connected to this concept with • Ω •, which represents "Ahu" which is "H". This stands for the Hardcore Realist, or Human Being. What this is beginning to say here is the Natural Person, is a Human being that has within it, the Hardcore Realist. This also has the number 9 connected to it with the letter "Ahu" having 1+11.2 connected to it. What I AM showing you is how to gather information on a concept and put it in its Mathematical arrangement. The Hardcore Realist is the Spirit MAN, and the Natural Person is the Natural Man. You add these 2 concepts together and you get a Human Being. Now, this Human Being has 11 stations, while only 1 individual entity. This 1 individual holding 11 stations has a contractive and expansive Generator we know as the tic of the heart, and the inhale and exhale connected to it. Hence, we have 1+11.2:

1. Natural Person/Human Being

+11 Stations

1. Integumentary System

2. Skeletal System
3. Muscular System
4. Nervous System
5. Endocrine System
6. Cardiovascular System
7. Lymphatic System
8. Respiratory System
9. Digestive System
10. Urinary System
11. **Reproductive System**

=

12. All 11 Systems together as 1 with the inhale-exhale as its Generating function - .2

This is not where it stops. Before one can say they are a Natural Person, the 11 stations must be defined and Comprehended as systems that we as the Consciousness that constructs Character through temperament Govern all in conjunction with Universal Law. Once we Comprehend how the Letter "Ahu" manifests 12.2 as a Human Being, we find that this says that a Natural Person, is the WORD and the Light. Naturally the process would continue with having to define the WORD and Light before it would manifest as a motion that never dies, traveling the journey of Light = 3.2. Now, the number 9 comes in. Nine deals in the Birth of a Human Being. Upon conception, Birth is the accurate effect at 9 months. The Human Being or Natural Person is born of the Mother Nuhfamuoh, making it manifest as the Word's Light through the ebb and flow of the **Infinite- Divine-Dual**ity = 12.2 = 9 + 3. Once the Circumstances of this are Comprehended, we know "Kebuk" - the Light of the WORD is Mason, born of the Mother with dual Tendencies. **The manifestation of Masons Born of the Mother are always known as**

the Traveling Man (3=1+2), with dual Tendencies (.2) in Motion through the 11 stations. Once you have developed an acute Comprehension of how to take a single concept and Mathematically psychologize it, you should then start to put them together and learn their meanings. **We just Mathematically deciphered that the Natural Person is a Traveling Man.** After this, learn to do the same with the opposite table.

Before giving the 1st degree Student Formula, I want to give short study, ready definitions to the terms for Students to take into the laboratory and dissect. I also request that each Student construct their own definitions to terms that learning may fit all Temperaments and perceptions of Reality.

PSYCHOMETRIC MATHEMATICAL TABLE OF DEFINITIONS

0_1 Macrocosmic ALL, or PI - The Pure Infinity of the unknowable indefinable Living MIND, Animating the Mentalism of the immeasurable Youniverse, calculating LIFE of All Microcosmic Mentalities of Consciousness. - $\circ$ = 360 or 3.14 22/7

1. The WORD - The Cosmic Musical combinations of Sound vibrating Pure Infinite Energy into the spheres of the Youniverse and surrounding Hosts as the Creative Mentalism of the ALL - The Cosmic harmonious creative energy vibrating its sound into the Youniverse, known by cosmic hosts as the Language of the GODS - $\in$ = 1,088

2. The Light, or Order - The Illuminations of Pure Infinity-Sound-LIFE-Animation- Mentalism. The Intellectual-Scientific-Lawful-Architectural-Mathematical and Spiritual data of Reality - The Consciousness that Radiates the Mentalism of the ALL - LIFE-In-GOD'S-Holy-Temple-Spiritual Awareness illuminating the Mental experiences of the Natural Structures of perception through the senses, manifesting Characteristics that Comprehend celestial and Natural Circumstances in balance - $\daleth$ = 186,000 or 3.360

3. Motion/Travel = Vibratory Force of Energy in every range frequency moving in particular calculated speeds. - The aggregate transitory energy amalgamated into mass, manifesting the vibratory trinity of vaporous gas that can slow down to form liquidy substance that can

slow down to form a solid frozen substance. The frozen solid substance can transition into high speeds of Force of Energy with heat to reverse the aggregation of solid into liquid and then gas/vapor - Mentalism-Animating-Navigation through the Radiant Youniversal Consciousness of the ALL - $\wedge = 34^{10}$

4. Elements/Square - The Height, Depth, Length, and Width of Over, Under, Inner, and Outer standings, balanced through degrees of Man's measured Character Comprehending Circumstances of Hardcore Reality. - the Sources of Equational Solution called Proton, Neutron, Electron, Weak Force, Strong Force, Electromagnetism and Gravity Structuring the variables of Molecular-Autonomical-Nucleus. The Temperamental Structures of Land, Water, Air and Fire, Conjuncted to the Seasonal structures of Spring, Summer, Fall, and Winter conjunctal to Hot, Cold, Wet and Dry of Man's standings. - Carbon, Hydrogen, Oxygen, Nitrogen, Calcium, Phosphorus, Chlorine, Sulfur, Sodium, Magnesium, Iodine and Iron; all square in Anatomical measurements. - $\sqcap = 90$

5. Time/Space - Areas, Distances and Speeds accelerated by Man's perception of Reality - The Authoritative Rule of the 4 dimensional standings calculated by the degree standings in Man's perceptual comprehension - the 7 measurements of Man's standing in Balance of Day and Night; 7. Morning, 6. High Noon, 5. After Noon 4. Evening 3. Night, 2. Mid Night, 1. Dawn. - The rotation of celestial hosts around the Star of Fire, making up years, months, weeks, days, hours, minutes, and seconds in Man's perception of Reality - Nature's Seasonal cycles of Vernal Equinox, Summer Solstice, Autumnal Equinox and Winter Solstice in conjunction with celestial rotation of hosts around the Star of Fire. - $\cup = 60$

6. Equilibrant Form - the manifestation of Pure Infinite Force into Man's Constitutional Order - The Balance of Thinking, Feeling and Willing in Motion with Character, Comprehension and Circumstances - the equilibrium of Spirit MAN and Natural Man as one - JL = 7/360

7. GOD-Consciousness - The Thinking System of Awareness that rises in degrees and squared on the right angle of MAN'S Standings in Length, Width, Depth and Height in 360° - The Light of Awareness manifesting as the Natural Man's Mental Guidance-Order-and-Directional Power - $\uparrow$ = 9/360 ÷ 7/360 = 12 6/7

8. Creation/Definition - the manifestation of GOD-Consciousness into Action, spoken through the WORD "BE", structured from MAN'S degree in standings - the Building Up of Order in All manifest motions - $\frown$ = 9

9. Natural Person - the flesh and blood living Human Being, integrated into Nature the Natural Mother with GOD-Consciousness - the SUN/Light/SON of the Mother/Matri/Matrix/Ma; Ma-SON = Mason. - The Mind with Mentalism Traveling Within the flesh and blood of the Molecules, with Autonomy in the Nucleus - Ω = 1+11.2

0_2 Microcosm of Macrocosm - the Hardcore Reality of ALLAH The Great I AM and Man being One. The Mastery of Spirit in MATTER, Governing Time and Creation of transcendental Consciousness dimensionally as the Great Intelligence of All Motion - $\diagup$ = 720 8 360/360 = 1 = 720

Before giving the Formula, I want to Be sure that Comprehension is valid regarding the Elemental Temperament of each Individual. Seeing the arrangements of the terms and their meanings, I must stress that calculations and Psychoanalysis vary according to the Temperament of the Individual. For those who may not know what Mansions are, or what Mansions they are from, or what kind of Elemental Temperament they may have, I will give a small chart as it is necessary to have and retain for Formulated Measurements. A Mansion is a zodiac house; and this is only a determinant of the month in which you were born, in this Student's degree. All constructive counting starts at the Spring/Vernal Equinox:

MANSIONS

1. Aries = Fire
2. Taurus = Land
3. Gemini = Air
4. Cancer = Water
5. Leo = Fire
6. Virgo = Land
7. Libra = Air
8. Scorpio = Water
9. Sagittarius = Fire
10. Capricorn = Land
11. Aquarius = Air
12. Pisces = Water

Temperament/Element

A Temperament is a distinguished behavioral Character, or Characteristics established through Human constitutions Elemental positions depending on one's time of birth. A Temperament can be sensitive, passionate, introverted, extroverted, passive, aggressive, insensitive, exaggerating and many others. When making Mathematical Assessments—regarding a Temper of an Individual, we must look at the Element of their Mansion and the language of the Element. Review the chart of Mansions and you'll see the Elements: Fire, Land, Air and Water connected to them. Each element distributes its disposition through the Natural Persons process (BHR 2:6-17). Within us All, these Temperaments in connection to the Elements are called Humors. They are: 1. Land/Melancholic, Phlegmatic/Water, Sanguine/Air, and Choleric/Fire. $\triangle$

1. Fire = Choleric (Aries, Leo, Sagittarius) - These Temperaments are strong Thinkers, very energetic, active, enthusiastic, passionate, outgoing, easygoing, friendly, humble, extroverted, soft spoken through expressive dialect, kind, strict, and can become angry or over excited very easily.

2. Land = Melancholic $\triangledown$ (Taurus, Virgo, Capricorn) - These Temperaments are practical, stable, emphatic on security, patient, industrious, strong willed, withstands long range goals, and is often quiet, withdrawn, can easily become sad, and is very comfortable in the materialisms acquired through work and existence.

3. Air = Sanguine $\triangle\!\!\!\!-$ (Gemini, Libra, Aquarius) - These Temperaments are very communicative, intelligent, like to deal in the mental plane, speaks and writes effectively and is often times carefree,

forgetful, unreliable, analytical and interested in the world and its ideas.

4. Water = Phlegmatic ▽ (Cancer, Scorpio, Pisces) - These Temperaments are emotional, intuitive, introverted, sensitive to surroundings, creative, empathetic, has good imagination, hidden depths, and is often detached, nonchalant, passive, mellow, pleasant, charming.

These are the Temperaments and their elemental connections to the Mansions.

When we go into the Real lesson books at a Student's degree, we are to combine this data with all of the data thus far given, in order to Realistically Psychologize this Math in the Book of Hardcore Reality. It is imperative to learn as I have given in this sample form, how to Psychologize the Math outside of the Formula and the equations in the Book of Hardcore Reality.

Your next assignment is to learn all that you can about the zodiac wheel of Mansions, Temperaments, Elements and their connections to Youniversal Law and the Psychometric Mathematics. Land and Water Temperaments are Contractive and Air and Fire Temperaments are expansive. **Before attempting to psychoanalyze another, the Student must be able to discern the Spatial Tendency of their Elemental Temperament within their own Youniverse.** Spatial Tendency is simply the communicated disposition of an Elemental Temperament through the Mansions Sacred Halls in the Youniverse. This is very important when on a quest for Self Knowledge. When discerning this portion of Math refer back to (BHR 2:6-19).

FORMULAS

There are 3 degrees in this Knowledge of Self Curriculum, consisting of 3

Stairs to climb Mathematically. Formulas are organized in degrees of **Arithmetic, Algebra** and **Geometry** for the Evolution of All initates Consciousness (BHR 4:48-49). Arithmetic is for a Student who learns. Algebra is for an Adept who discerns. And Geometry, is for a Master who Serves. No degrees in Formula should be mixed together.

Degree #1 Student Formula

$S = (MD) + \text{Columns} \cdot \text{Sum}$

Mansion times the Digit, plus the Columns, times the Sum manifests (=) a Solution.

We'll meet again in the Lesson Book #1 for a Student, with the breakdown, and utilization of this Formula. In the meanwhile, Master the assignment given in this portion of Sample form and start your Journey in the BHR and in general.

THE ALPHABET OF AKH-HULEBUK

Today, the popularity of ignorance dominates the perceptual outlook of the People. The Creative spark has been tainted by subliminal commercial advertising, to see the Building of destruction as legitimate. What I mean by that, is the representatives of the Elder generation and our generation that are out front with/in some form of potential leadership, advertise the necessity for mass accumulations of inanimate materialism, inanimate sociability, counterproductive education and many other disqualifying traits; the Building of Destruction. The big time corporations, politicians, record labels and what have you, use the People to promote the mechanics of Destruction to the younger generation. Resultantly, everything is a party, everything is a joke, everything is fun and nothing of worth is relevant in this existence. Unbeknownst to their tainted psyches, the advertisers get paid to educate them in the Science of Destruction; and they, in turn, become targets of a bigger scheme they have no idea functions in the manner that it does. When our youth exhibit destructive Characteristics in society, they become targeted by the New Era Corporate Slavery System. They have no clue of such a thing being in existence, or being the big time business that it is. For those who may not know, the Criminal Justice System is the New Era Corporate Slavery System. The business of incarceration is big when concerning the denationalized destructive youth.

For any who may think I'm making this up as just an opinionated theory, review the following:

> "Neither slavery, nor involuntary servitude, except as a

punishment for crime whereof the party shall have been duly convicted, shall exist within the United States, or any place subject to their jurisdiction."

U.S. Constitution

Section 1 Amendment #13

This is no class or lesson in/on law, so we'll make this brief and tie it in to the point. Trained perceptual outlooks have been conditioned to think that slavery has been outlawed. Such cannot be further-further-further from the Truth. When reviewing the dead badge of law, we find that slavery and involuntary servitude does in fact exist when/if one is convicted of a crime.

The language and its arrangement are meant to throw you off. Analyze the arrangement of words: 'neither slavery, nor involuntary servitude EXCEPT AS A PUNISHMENT FOR CRIME SHALL EXIST! Can you see it now? Is it clear? The slavery of today is in the Criminal Justice System. Think ... the advertising of destruction helps promote and encourage destructive Thinking, that in turn produces destructive behavior. Destructive behavior is called crime. Destructive people are called criminals.

"Crime - an act committed, or omitted, in violation of law, forbidding or commanding it and for which punishment is imposed upon conviction. - Unlawful activity. - A serious moral offense. - An unjust senseless act or condition.

"Criminal - Guilty of crime. - disgraceful: shameful - one who has committed or been legally convicted of a crime."

180

Webster's II New College Dictionary

Are you seeing the connection? It benefits the legal system when we or our youth show disdain for Order. Right this moment, the profile, street vernacular, dress code and lack of Real Education is getting someone criminalized. What is it about all of this that makes it so in the open while yet so mis-Comprehended? The language of it all is the portion many lack Comprehension of. This puts it in an educational venue. The popularizing of ignorance keeps one at a disadvantage in this world. The youth know nothing about slavery, it's venue of the past, it's meaning, what it done to our People, and how it functions today because the trained advertisers and potential leaders who are out front representatives of Us say the past is the past. They say they are not those People, and the descendents of the monsters who ran those industries are not the monsters their People are. When it comes to communicating Reality, Truth and Order to our youth, we seem to - as a collective group of people, lack the social skills, education and charisma to constructively bring balance to the youth's instabilities. Am I saying that our youth's issues of ignorance, stupidity and foolishness reflect bad on us as adults and elders today? Yes!

I AM saying that we are responsible for their Thinking, perception, education, future, protection from harm and so much more. Our communication skills, our education, our Thinking, perception and retention of information are off.

All we show our youth is division; how to argue, debate and be anti-social, how to be weak, ignorant and foolish, and how to utilize being 'Black' as a means to fail. This is why I'm so against arguing, debating, combat with words, being opinionated, and all vile, rash representations of chaos. None of these traits educate the youth to have balance; these traits deteriorate their psyches into hopelessness, carelessness, and ultimately into crime.

Sociology is a requirement when Thinking along the lines of solution. The fields of sociometry and sociolinguistics are keys to bringing solutions to our ongoing issues of destruction. Our communicating skills are not up to par as adults today. We are scattered all over the place when it comes to our means of conversing. Some use street vernacular (ebonics, dead hip hop lingo), some use the Caucasian News Anchor lingo, some use the attorney and politician lingo, some use the Baptist preacher lingo, some use the prison lingo, and some are normal and use plain English. The thing about this English language is, it is not taught with any linguistic form.

This is why it can be all over the place, while all being in the same system of communicating. One of the things about Ancient Systems of Education, was the discipline of communicating. The means of making known information was done at strict levels. There were hieroglyphs that translated messages with various meanings. There were verbal signals, sounds and frequencies of sound that meant something in particular. There was body language and signs that had various translations in art. With all of this being a part of the educational system, order was manifest in the means of exchanging discourse. There was no arguing, debating, or combat with words. It wasn't necessary to do any such thing amongst one another, because such a thing did not co-opt Comprehension.

When you think about it, the Business Structures and their representatives are linguistically sound. They know their business. They know how to communicate on a level that you and I may not Comprehend on the surface. We are all supposed to talk the same language. Truth is, we don't. There is an initiated means of communicating English, and there's an uninitiated means. We speak the uninitiated English language today. We don't want to cry and protest about the problem, we want to present solutions to the problem. Ancient concepts of language surrounded putting meaning to each sign that represented a verbal sound.

As the initiate learned to speak, there was a basis to the sounds being made that could be Intellectually, Scientifically, Lawfully, Architecturally and Mathematically broken down. Once this was done, the initiate was to connect the sound and its sign to Character. Every sound and sign made at that point could be explained as a part of the initiate's Character, that connects to the forces of Nature, that connects to the cosmic expansions. This is beginning to being taught the linguistic form of communication. It is then that sounds can be put together to make words that represent a power to control motion.

This is where we are lacking. What I have done, is constructed a linguistic system that you can call your own, for you to begin to learn one step at a time. There are 26 Alphabets that relates to the English alphabet. Each alphabet has a sound and a meaning to go with its name. The responsibility of the People is to go back to the Mental State of our Ancestor's Moral Standings. Before starting to put sounds together to make words, we start at the beginning by learning the alphabet, its sounds, its meanings and the Mathematical concept ascribed to it. Before I give an illustration, let s look at the Alphabet, its sounds and the meanings thereof.

Sound	Alphabet

Ah -

= Ahlē: ALL, ALLAH, or Animate "A" - The Macrocosmic Everything of All in manifest; the Everything of what appears to Be Nothing in All things. - The Microcosm of the Macrocosm. - The imparted Motion of spirit and activity into Thought. = $360,720 - 8\frac{360}{360} = 1$

nuh -

= Nūhlē: Body "B" - The entire material structure and substance of an organism esp. of a Human Being = 33.11

hu -

= Bālē: Consciousness or Chaos "C" - Aware of existence sensation enviroment and Thought. Capable of Thinking, Feeling, Willing, perceiving and deciding within existence, environment and structure. - The boundlessness, darkness, uncalculated motion that can cause confusion. = 5.360 or 0^3.

mu -

= Mūlē: Degree - one of a series of steps or stages in a process "D" = $3\ 90/360$

le -

= Lezi: Evolution "E" - To evolve; a gradual process in which something changes and morphs into Balance, order and degree. = 3.9

akh -

= Lēakh: Family "F" - a fundamental social group consisting of males and females and their offspring. = 2

ra -

= Rālē God or Government "G" - The degree rising Mentalism of Order that Radiates Light and facilitates structure and Reason through Temperament: the illumination of Principle through the Natural Man. - The Legislative, Executive and Judicial Rules of Natural Authority that constructs, enforces and translates All-Law; the Generating-Operating-Distributing Power Of the People, By the People and For the People. = 7

eh -

= Ahū: Hardcore Realist or Human "H" - The Motion of the Reality of Spirit; the WORD of the ALL. - The Natural Person of Elemental Structure in aggregate design. The WORD manifest in the Natural Person giving Individuality in existence. The traveler through elemental structure. = 360 or 1+11.2

yah -

= Yahlē: ISLAM or Hotep "I" - The Infinite Sounds of Light Animating Mentalism Motions; the Intelligence of Science Law Architecture and Mathematics that gives the inner workings of the Natural Person the Building mechanics of Infrastructure Symbolism Labor in and through the Ancestral Morale; Three Fold system designed for the Natural Person to Learn, Discern and Know Thyself; from Whence All-Law manifest, that gives form to the Life we exist in. - The Light of the WORD; the Hardcore Reality in the Order of Time to bring Evolution through the Balance of Pure Infinite Energy. - The Lawful Architectural Mathematical Basis of Hardcore Reality; the Gift of PEACE - Productive Education Activating Cosmic Energy. = 3/360 or 1

sh -

= Shāh: Judge "J" - A Government official authoritatively deciding upon the

Rule of Order in All cosmic and Natural measurements. = 9

duh -

= Dūhāh: Knowledge "K" - Science gained through experienced activity. - To Know. - Comprehension acquired through perception by Intellect, translasting a balance in standings through the senses.

buk -

= Lēbuk: Light or Love "L" - Electromagnetic Radiation of fire; the Luminosity or brilliance of Consciousness providing awareness and perception to the Natural Person; the Guiding Official Divinely present in All Natural Persons, as the innate Consciousness and perceiver of every tense - past, present and future. - the Guided Official's Divine Mercy, compassion, care, benevolence, service and sacrifice exhibited and extended to the Wight Race; the Sacrificial service of Order that constructs Order in Thinking, perceiving activity and future manifestation. The 1st Principle of the GOD-Consciousness in Man. = 186,000, or 1

Ke -

= Lēkē: Mentalism or Matriarch "M" - The Infinite Reality accelerating the Motion of Formula and Principle that constructs Youniversal Intelligence of Thought, creation and order. The telepathic dimensional energy of cosmic order, constructing the Principles of Law and balance. - The Mother Principle; the actual substance of Thought, matter or material substance. $= 34^{10}$ or 8

bu -

= Lēbū: Navigation "N" - To plan, record and control the position and course of Motion through Man's standings. To voyage through the Natural Land, Waters, Air and Fire as the Light of the WORD. = 4 7/12

fa -

= Fāmah: Order "O" - The standard arrangement of Balance amongst competent parts that proper functions of Law and Formula may manifest; organization within and throughout Nature, cosmic expansion, Humanity and its stations of function. - ISLAM; the Operative Guild of natural persons, structurally Building Balance from the

Blue Print of All-Law. = 3.360

he -

= Hēlē: PI "P" ~ Pure Infinity of Hardcore Reality; a transcendental number representing the ratio of the circumference to the diameter of a circle and appearing as a constant in a wide range of mathematical calculations = 3.14, 22/7

ish -

= Māh: Quadrant "Q" - a quarter; a circular arc subtending a central angle: one-fourth of the circumference of a circle. = 90°

leh -

= Ahlehlē: Ruler "R" - A Sovereign Rule of Order in the cosmic National and Natural expansion =17/9

ba -

= Lēbā: Sound or Sign "S" - A vibratory articulation mentally auditory, and heard in a series of frequences extended from the Spirit of Hardcore Reality; free from moral defect; the vibrations of the WORD Traveling in ranges measurable by comprehension of All-Law. - The evidence suggesting the presence of a fact, condition or quality in the Natural. = 1,088, or

lu -

= Lūlē: Time "T" - Duration; a non-spatial continuum in which events occur in apparently irreversible succession from the past through the present Moment to the Future; Areas, distances and Speeds accelerated by Man's perception of Reality = 60, 24/60

zi -

= Ōh: Youniverse or Universe "U" - All existing things from the uncountable Galaxies Ozones and Dimensional Stars of cosmic expansion and Mental Reality, as well as the Natural land and Humanity at large. The ALLs Mentalism that is bounded in Order and constructs the Intelligence of Individualism. =1 7/360

gu -

= Gūlē: Vision "V" - Intelligent sight structuring acute perception and Square discernment; the mental image formed by perceptual sight. = 2/360 mah -

= Muzi: Wisdom or Womb "W" - Square Standings on Principles. What is Right and Real; Gained Obtained Developed experience that constructs a walk down the narrow path; the Learning acquired in the Sacred Halls from the Youniversity of ISLAM - The Dark Matter of The Youniverse that gives birth to Motion and material substance. = 9

ex -

= Lēex; Unknown "X" - an unidentified situation, set of Circumstances or concept. =

oh -

= Māyah; LWAF - Land, Water, Air, Fire "Y" - The fundamental Forces that compose the aggregation of material substance that makes Temperamental humors align with the Nature of Existence. = 4 90/360

iz -

= Izlē: Zodiac or Zeal "Z" - A band of the celestial sphere, encompassing the paths of the principal Planets, the moon and the sun, the celestial band divided into

12 astrological signs, each 30° wide, and
named after constellations - Enthusiasm
and devotion to a cause. = 12

After seeing the Alphabetical arrangement, we should better
Comprehend that, the initiates Journey into Learning a language and how
to make it our own.

As shown, there are steps in processing information regarding the
structure of this linguistic form. This is more than A to Z with sounds
that make words.

Take the letter "• ⌣ • - Lēakh" for example. The sound to this
sign/Alphabet/symbol is "akh," and means the fundamental social group
consisting of males and females, and their offspring. Before the initiate
could utilize this sound to connect to other sounds that make words, one
must make the connection to the concept. What this means is find the
relevance of the concept within.

Knowing that you are Infinite-Divine-Dual by Nature, how do you find
within yourself the fundamentals of sociometry? What is fundamental?
What is Sociometric and self? This is one of the Key ingredients to
learning. Fundamental is something that is significant; sociometry is the
quantitative study of interpersonal relationships in a population especially
study and measurement of preferences; and Self is the Natural person.
Hence, this is a study of the significant interpersonal relationship with the
Spirit MAN and the Natural Man. We are to learn everything there is to
learn about Youniversal Law and our inner stations. We know that we
came from Atom and Evolution. Atom is male, Evolution is female.
From these 2, comes the offspring that makes the inner stations one big
family (BHR 2:28-31). From these male and female "cells", comes the

male and female x and y chromosomes. This goes on and on until the Natural Man, is in balance as a Family within the Spirit MAN. Once this is Comprehended, the outer aspect could be analyzed. This is how All of the Alphabets are to Be learned. Once done, the next step is to learn the math ascribed to the symbol. 2 is connected to "Lēakh", which implies the Spirit MAN and Natural Man, the Dual Tendencies of Light and Darkness, Atom and Evolution, Organic and Inorganic compounds, the X and Y chromosomes, contractive and expansive stations connected to our Elemental make up, our Natural Mother and Father and so on. Not only are we to learn this, we are to learn the True structure and Order of everything we grasp. Then, make a connection with the information, its sociometric quantities, Youniversal Law, Natural Law, the ascribed Math and the Book of Hardcore Reality. Take your time when dealing with the Alphabet.

We desire for you to grasp the concept as it was composed for your Gaining Obtaining Developing Consciousness. The chart that is made with just the Alphabet sound and Symbol, is for the practice of the initiate after learning the first steps explained. Every sound, meaning, symbol and concept should be mastered.

Alphabet Sound Name

	Alphabet	Sound	Name
A =		ah	Ahlē
B =		nuh	Nuhlē
C =		hū	Bālē
D =		mū	Mūlē
E =		lē	Lēzi
F =		akh	Lēakh
G =		ra	Rālē
H =		eh	Ahū

I =   yah   Yahlē

J =   sh   Shāh

K =   duh   Dūhāh

L =   buk   Lēbuk

M =   kē   Lēkē

N =   bū   Lēbū

O =   fa   Fāmah

P =   hē   Hēlē

Q =   ish   Māh

R =		leh	Ahlehlē
S =		ba	Lēbā
T =		lū	Lūlē
U =		zi	Ōh
V =		gū	Gūlē
W =		mah	Muzi
X =		ex	Lēex
Y =		oh	Māyah
Z =		iz	Izlē

The next step is to learn the concept of putting words together and putting sounds together. This Alphabet reads from Right to Left and is utilized in various ways. Putting words together is an agronomic arrangement that consists of the meanings to the terms ascribed to the Alphabet. Putting sounds together is making a word from the English Language:

Putting Words Together

> "The circumference of the Area was called "Faluizzi•" which meant the Authoritative Cosmic Order of Time, structured in the Zodiac Mansions of Mentalism in the Universe."

> -BHR 1:78

What you see is the Sounds of words put together representing the words:

Order-Time-Zodiac-Universe = Fa-lu-iz-zi.

In the Book of Hardcore Reality, you'll know when you come across those kinds of arrangements, when you see a dot (•) next to the term. If you wanted to write this with the Alphabet, you'd start from right to left -

To break down the verse, the initiate would have had to master the alphabet from the student's degree of instructions given thus far and define circumference and Area. The next step would be for the initiate to add the Mathematics of the Alphabet together that brings about a sum, and start the Journey into the Psychometric Mathematical Analysis:

Fa=3.360, Lu=60, Iz=12, Zi=7/360

Mastering the Alphabet comes with Comprehending the Math ascribed to the concept. There are 3 degrees in this Educational venture, each making 360°; Time is measured in 60 second intervals; there are 12 Zodiac Mansions and 7 Eyes of ALLAH, 7 Hills, 7 Equational Solutions all symbolically equal to 360°. The manifest is 75 7/360. Psychometrically, this says GOD-Consciousness in Time and Space with the Great GOD of the Universe over the Motions of Equilibrant form of the Microcosm. This is something we'll get into outside of the Sample format. Anytime you put words together, follow these steps.

Putting Sounds Together

When saying a Word itself, you make the Word with the sounds and not the Alphabet. The symbols could be used however, when putting sounds together:

"The inscription read:

Keahbu-Dūhāh•-Nuhlē• /

and it meant MAN, Know Thyself.

It was the only Way that the Masters Key was reachable, that opened the Portal

Doors into Faluizzi and beyond."

-BHR 4.44

Look at the inscription. Remember that the Alphabetical symbols read from right to left. What we are looking at, is the sounds making a word - Keahbu;

This says MAN, Ke = M, ah = A, bu = N. There's no Math with this.

Remember that this is yours to have. Learn it the way I'm explaining, and learn it your own way also. When wanting to communicate with the language, put sounds together to make Words, and use the name of the Alphabet when wanting to say an already made word - Keahbu = MAN, Dūhāh• = Knowledge, Nuhlē• = Body = Self. Outside of this sample lesson, we will give you step by step ways to learn this language and dissect the Book of Hardcore Reality. This is for our Building one another up with something constructive, that we may teach the youth how to learn themselves and speak a language that is untampered with. We'll see you in Lesson Book #1 in Linguistics.

SAMPLE LESSON

I sat for a few days pondering over how to start this sample lesson. This was very hard to decide upon, due to my sincerity and intentions of being effective with the words that I use to encourage study. So I decided to come in a way that the majority can relate to.

First, I'm a Hardcore Realist. Before I'm anything else, I'm Real. I don't pretend to be something that I AM not, nor do I try fitting into groups, circles, cliques or clubs. Along the lines of my existence up to this Present Moment, I didn't always stand firm in the confidence of my Reality. I had to learn the hard way that there are only 2 kinds of Circumstances that we all have to be Conscious of; one is Real and one is fake. As simple as I put it, is as simple as it is. This can take you a long way if you learn to keep it at the front of your Thoughts. There's a way in existence that we can travel and deal in fiction. Along the journey, you'll witness Real People and fake People, while put in a position to yourself, Be Real, or fake. I know that this is an unorthodox style and approach to composing a lesson, but just bear with me and follow the point I'm trying to make.

I've been incarcerated in physical prison for going on 15 years. This is a fiction world closed in by a wall, holding both the Real and fake Characters. Prison is a modern day slave plantation designed to break the Mental capacity to Be Real, down into an institutionalized animal. You have one of two choices in a dismal situation as such. You can either Be strong and endure through the psychological assaults inflicted upon the psyche by Being Real, or you can Be Weak and succumb to the institutional politics, culture, ignorance and games by Being fake. One is a Leader, Pace Setter and Conscious Realist, and the other one is a follower, send off person, and is hunted by insecurities, guilt and illusion. In this place, I've been tried on various levels. Due to being a Realist, I've been called strict, militant, too serious, not a fun guy to be around, too sensitive, eccentric, one who Thinks I'm better than everyone else, weird, a bug, and many other things that I won't write on this manuscript. At first, I couldn't fathom why so much negative energy was being shot at me. Within the first 7 years, I used to try defending my stand on what's Right and Real. I honestly couldn't Comprehend how the People around me weren't taking their Circumstances seriously. My Uncle Skeet assured me that in a place like this (prison), carelessness, weakness, tribalism, savagery, and hatred are the key ingredients that make up the fake, phony, smile in your face, and knife you in the back, dispositions portrayed by the Characters surrounding me. I was instructed to stay consistent in sorting out my Complications and be Real in my approach to making decisions.

In that field, I had to continue looking backwards to see how much damage I caused People in my fake and weak state of mind. I couldn't continue forward in formulating the basis of a Sincere and Real Solution without admitting to myself that: I'd done a lot of things wrong, hurt a lot of people, was gone in darkness, screwed my existence up, left my baby Ahlexis Andreya and her Mother Brandi to suffer, my nieces and nephews, my brother, my Mother and family at large. I started to see how my Grandparents worked every day, never hung out, never got into trouble, and raised my Mother and her siblings to have that value system of hard work and belief in what's Real, and grow old into wisdom and Divine Love. I started to see how my Uncles, Aunties and Mother followed those values, had my cousins and me, and they raised us to have the same values. I noticed how I disrupted the "Parham culture" by going against the values and coming to prison. Such a thing was a disrespect to the hard work my Grandparents, their Parents, and my

Mother, Aunties and Uncles put in, that I could be afforded the many great opportunities that were presented to me. Yes! I began to see how fake, phony, disrespectful, careless, immature, ignorant and one-sided I was. I began to Realize, that my choices, my disobedience, my lack of awareness, values and morals, damaged my perception of Reality. Coming to grips with these and many other ills about my own self was by far one of the hardest things I ever had to do.

When I did, though, I was finally able to Comprehend how I ended up in prison.

Two full years straight, I apologized to my Mother for my insubordination, my Uncle and all who would listen, and humbled myself to receive instruction.

Now I know you're wondering why I'm explaining all of this to you, and what it has to do with the lessons at hand. **I want you to see about me, that I couldn't travel the path of Real, until I was able to see how fake I was.**

It was only after dealing with my own insufficiencies, flaws, admitting error and accepting fault that I became humbled and willing to deal with the consequences in strength. At this moment, I want you to do the very same thing. Look back at who you were. Can you see that far, or have you suppressed the past? How ready are you to deal in Reality? Can you admit that perhaps you've been consumed by a fiction for a long time, which plays on the imbalance in the way that you make current decisions? How did your past affect your Present Moment? Where are you? Why? Is it Real or fake?

> "Reality - Dealing in What's real. - Not imaginary, fictional or pretend - The sum of all that is absolute, real

and unchangeable."

"Fiction - A lie - something accepted as fact without real justification merely for the sake of convenience: - an imaginative creation of literature comprising works of this kind: - assumed, in order to deceive: not genuine."

When we deal with our immediate Circumstances, we must look back on our past to decipher our conduct, decisions and how these things may have had bad effects on others. Although the past is unchangeable, it is also decipherable and set to reveal itself to any who may be willing to be Real. When you look back, it is not meant for you, me, or anyone to try changing things. Looking back deals in making preparation to move forward, when doing so from this angle. Before we do any work together, let's look at some of our errors as a collective core of People.

If we can be honest with ourselves, we'll willingly admit to the participation in, and partial creation of, the chaos within the current culture. In our past, we've done drugs, drank alcohol, fought one another, rebelled against our authority, practiced promiscuity, and many other vile things we've called being teenagers, or just having fun. We done all of this stuff in public, creating the idea in the observant youth of that times psyche, what was cool, uncool, acceptable, unacceptable, the perceptual outlook on Reality and fiction. In our ignorance, we had no idea ourselves about what was Real and/or fake.

The motivation behind a lot of mass bad decision making was consumption of money. Today, we may be very well aware of the fact that "legal tender/Federal Reserve Notes/U.S. Currency is just as fake as Monopoly money, but have failed to collectively guard and protect our youth with a Real Education regarding this fact. We in fact collectively continue on in our chase for the "dollar", brewing in the selfish, wreckless, careless, one-sided culture it creates.

There is failure on our parts to change the dynamics of our collective Circumstances which ultimately creates the pattern of failure in which our youth travel.

Remember Uncle Skeet's advice; he said to stay consistent in sorting out my own complications, and be Real in my approach to making decisions. As a collective people, this is something we must do as individuals and together.

This is the only way to productively change things, and protect the youth from the snares set that they have no idea exist around the culture, and within the culture of fiction. This is why I wanted to share with you how I had to look back on my own ignorance, and come to grips with Reality. This is something that we'd have to go through together.

I know that our pasts are not the same experiences. Due to us all having different Temperaments, we may have experienced some of the same situations, but perhaps had different perceptions of the experiences that may have caused different means of making decisions. We've all been in situations that caused for decisions based on Reality to manifest that we couldn't execute. Myself, for example, I was in a situation where I knew that Ahlexis Andreya was on her way into manifest. I was so blinded by my own ignorance, that I couldn't see destruction at the center of my decision making system. If I was in my right Mentalism, there's no way I would have done anything to jeopardize this beautiful young lady having a Father in her existence. If I were in any mental shape to Comprehend the Circumstances of parenting, then I'd have had more respect for my Elders - the parents of my generation, and for myself as a parent. There would have been no way that I would have ever disrespected Brandi in the many ways that I did. She's the Mother of Ahlexis Andreya, that I left for prison. Do you see how crazy this sounds? What Man in his right Mind leaves his family for prison, the streets, promiscuous affairs, gangs, or any reason? There was definitely a lack of Comprehending Reality, and being Real on my part. This applies to many good Brothers in Prison Right now! This applies to many good Sisters in Prison Right now! This applies to people who are out in the streets, struggling with dealing in making decisions from a Realist angle. All People are either going to choose to be Real or be fake. Some want to be Real and lack the Comprehension of doing so, while others just don't care either way. Together, we've stayed divided in our differences. Consequently, our children are the new targets for a world built around chaos, fiction, destruction, selfishness, carelessness, violence and everything that harms. Here's a sample look at what kind of lessons will come from this Order of Real Education.

Today, it may be a proven fact that many don't Comprehend the direction of Reality and its Order. When dealing in the Order of Reality, we should all intend to focus our abilities of Thinking and Reasoning, on how to make decisions and with logic in matters around what is factual and Real. This should Be All of our intentions. Now, when dealing in the Order of Reality that is Hardcore, we are projecting upright activities of Intelligence structured in Science, founded in Law, Raised in Architecture, explained through the exact Formulas of Mathematics. This is our culture. As we begin in this introductory course of study and building, we want to shed light on a few things that all Students should learn. What we want to do here is give a look into the Thinking and decision making system of a Hardcore Realist.

Fiction, as we Learned, is something that is not Real. It is a lie; an imaginative creation of literature comprising works of imagination. Fiction is deception and known as ingenuine. Ask yourself: "is this something that is going on in my surroundings? Have I been deceived by imaginative creations of literature?"

Comprehend, that everything outside of Nature and its constructive forces in your very surroundings, is fiction. Corporate Governments - Ordinances - Departments, entertainment, fortune 500 industries, municipalities, commerce and all things connected to all such commercialisms, are mere fictions that are imaginative creations of literature comprising works of imagination.

They only exist on paper. These fictions are brought into manifest by the activities of people and are mere ideas, Thoughts, and visions of deception that structures how a commercial fiction world should function. Is this right, wrong, a problem, harmless, or anything Just? This is a definite problem, wrong and unjust, when the many that function in the commercial world of fiction are unaware of the differences between Reality and fiction. Get this:

You are, I AM, We are, part and portion of the forces of Nature. **Like Nature and its forces, anything constructed outside of your very being is in fact, a fiction.** This is a very important concept to grasp in order to Comprehend the culture of a Hardcore Realist. Like the big corporations that were constructed to govern commerce and commercial governmental affairs, there is an artificial/fiction corporation, created to represent you and me in the commercial world and its governmental affairs. Remember that all corporate fictions only exist on paper. This is so important to begin Comprehending, because it is the beginning to removing the veil of delusional perception. What this means, is there is a flesh and blood Natural Person, and there's an artificial person that only exists on paper:

Artificial person/fiction/corporation

ANDRELL JASON PARHAM

Natural Person/Reality/flesh & blood

Andrell Jason Parham Bey©™ ©™

The fiction called ANDRELL JASON PARHAM is a corporate entity that exists on paper. The paper is a bond called Birth Certificate. The tracking numbers of this corporate fiction are the bond numbers on the certificate, and the Social Security numbers called Tax Identification Numbers. In Reality, the ANDRELL JASON PARHAM that has all caps for a name, can only be found on paper as a corporation [When we get into our Real Lesson books, we'll cover the grounds from A to Z about this]. The Natural Person, **Andrell Jason Parham Bey©™ ©™** is the Reality of a National Trademark representing Nature, the forces of Nature and flesh and blood Human Being/Wight Man (means what a Real Human Being is that was re-constructed as "white man" through the reconstruction period of history.) Did you know that your birth certificate was a bond/contract representing a corporate fiction that has a name just like your name? Did you know that in a fiction world, fiction Authority can only deal with fiction contracts? Did you know that you become a surety for the fiction by answering to/for it? Did you know that until you become the Secured Party Creditor of the fiction, you have no say in paying the fictions debts? Listen, as long as the fiction around us is considered Real to you, you'll never Comprehend the Circumstances we are all in due to fraud, deception, unawareness and theft. Until we collectively Realize that All corporate structures - from government to Merchants/Banks to municipalities to legal systems to unions, to artificial persons/strawmen/vessels/Corporations are only the business of commerce and they are fictions, then our Thinking, reasoning, how to make decisions and exercise of logic in all matters, will never change. This is why Reality is necessary to learn and function in.

Generationally, Reality was washed from our base of collective building.

The base to any structure is the foundation thereof, and all things are built from that grounding. We were "trained" by corporate advertising to be blind antisocial animals, lacking accurate perception of what's Real. We were conditioned to Think of the commercial world, as the standard when pondering the idea of successful roads. We were programmed through/by Public School curriculums, Television, brainwashed parental facilitating and entertainment at large, to think of productivity as going to school, getting a high school diploma, getting a job, getting married, having "kids", purchasing a house, a dog and a vehicle, then living happily ever after in a commercial world. People are really "trained" to think of this as success, and are willing to risk social stability with family, a Nationality, a status of Human recognition, love, order, respect and all things dealing in the Natural order of Motion. Many fall victim to the commercial scandals and have become obedient, voting, taxpaying, 14th Amendment citizens, who are denationalized, and only recognized as sureties to/for fiction/artificial persons. Remember that the base to any structure is its foundation, and all things are built from such a grounding. The base of this pattern of Thinking, Reasoning, decision making and logic dealing in this selfish, shrewd, careless, reckless, antisocial Character is in fact fiction and commercial. Everything built upon this base is an act of trickery.

The "training" comes in when parents stay in the complacency of fiction, teaching their children the chaos of this culture. They display selfish, greedy, antisocial Characteristics, seeking to accumulate a mass of materialism, while pushing away from Reality. This is their "training". Only animals can be "trained" to perform specific acts; and these animals are documented as registered property of Human Beings. **No Natural Person can be "Trained", or "conditioned" by any such scandal unless they themselves are the subjects of commercial conditioning.** The training is seen in parents raising **"kids"** rather than raising **"Human children." A "Kid" is an animal, a baby goat. A goat is a devil, or a representative of something considered bad.** To raise up **"kids/baby goats/animals"** is to train/condition an infant perception and utilization of senses to instinctively survive in a material world with mass consumptions of material gain, minus any awareness of Reality. Consequently we have a generation of current "kids", who are selfish, greedy, instinctive, trained animals thriving on consumption of materialism, for the means of survival with no sense of being a Human Being, Comprehending the Circumstances of Reality and fiction. We have given birth to a generation under us who have the same fictional value system. Hence, people kill, lie, cheat, mistreat, plot, scheme, rob and all acts of harmful, damaging mindlessness, for the fictitious perception of mass material gain.

At this Student stage and stair, we don't want to go too far off into exposing fiction because - without Conscious development, such unveilings can stir up the wrong kind of sentiments. We want to help construct order out of chaos, not flare up Temperaments into boundless passions. So, what we want to touch on here is the **Student degree** meanings to certain things in the **B**ook of **H**ardcore **R**eality that you may begin to Comprehend a basis of study from the removing of the veil from facts. Remember that the meanings to things rise in degree.

We're going to sample some things for you, that may seem complicated, but are not. Yon are an up and coming student of **I**ntelligence-**S**cience-**L**aw-**A**rchitecture-and-**M**athematics. This is about you and me learning together about ourselves and the connection we have in/to Reality.

> "Let Man Comprehend the Circumstances: We as The Natural Man do not live Life because we as Spirit MAN are The Life/Hardcore Realists; and Life lives through the Soul within the Natural Man."

> -BHR 9:38

Let's first look at MAN. There are 3 different perceptual ingredients to MAN, when Thinking within the realm of Reality. There's the Spirit MAN, there's the Soul of MAN and there's the Natural Man. The 3 are really 1 when we are in tune with the facts. We are in fact, MIND, Soul and Body, all intertwined into 1 functioning entity. When we say Spirit MAN, we are referring to the **P**ure **I**nfinity **in the expansion of THE ALL**. This is Hardcore Reality (BHR 1:5). The Hardcore Reality that is the Pure Infinity of THE ALL is MIND.

The Mind is the unlimited Everything that is the Life. Life is eternal; holding no beginning and no ending and is everywhere. The Mind is the Hardcore Realist that constructs the Youniverse in which it lives. This is due to its Creative "Mentalism – Animation – and - Navigation in Spirit."

> "Mentalism - Intellectual capacities. Thinking."

> "Animate - to give and impart life and/or spirit to with Motion."

> "Navigate - To control the course of."

"**M**entalism – **A**nimating - **N**avigation - The controlled course of the Motions of Life through Intellectual capacities of Spiritual Thinking."

When we say Spirit MAN, we are referring to the controlled Motions of Life, through the course of Intellectual capacities in Spiritual Thinking. Hence, it is an **I**ntelligence of Spiritual Thought, **A**ll **M**otioned in the construction of the Youniverse. So, what we are saying here is that THE ALL is your/my MIND: the Youniverse is Mentalism. The Mentalism of the Thinking of the Mind is Pure Infinite Energy. This is an everlasting Life and lives through the other 2 factual orders of MAN. When we say Soul of MAN, we are referring to the Consciousness that makes the Present Moment Real (BHR 5:33-35).

> "Conscious - aware of one's own thoughts, sensations, existence and environment"

> "Present - The period in time intermediate between past and future - At hand."

> "Moment - The particular period of importance."

"**Soul-of-Man** - The particular period of importance intermediate between past and future that is the at hand Awareness of Thought, sensation and existence in any specific environment."

When we say Soul-of-MAN, we're referring to an at hand moment of awareness of one's own Thinking, Feeling and Will through the existence of any specific environment. MAN - which is the Hardcore Realist, or Mind has a Thinking capacity that experiences an Awareness of Self (Itself) through the environment of its Youniverse. The Present Moment of Awareness is **the I**ntellectual knowledge of **A**ll **M**otions manifest in the Youniversal environment. We call this Consciousness, the Soul, as it perceives through its awareness the Purpose of Feeling, of Reason and of decision making. Through this 2nd factual ingredient of MAN, does all preponderant vision emerge, that I AM - **The Intelligence of All Motion**, may be Cultivated through decisive, Conscious decision making of creation. The only Reality is the Present Moment. Tomorrow has yet to exist in manifest and yesterday no longer accounts to manifestation. Although we are able to look back into yesterday to prepare for tomorrow, neither are the Present Moment. Right now, at hand, is what the Soul-of-MAN is Conscious of - in Feeling, Reasoning, and decision making. The Soul-of-MAN cannot adjust yesterday into a different manifestation or predict tomorrow to be a specific kind of manifestation. It is through this at hand measurement of time, that the Soul-of-MAN becomes the Ruler of the 3rd ingredient; only when in Balance with Hardcore Reality. This 3rd ingredient through which MAN travels, is the Natural environment called the Natural Man, Molecular-Autonomical-Nucleus.

> "Molecular - A stable configuration of atomic nuclei and electrons bound together by electrostatic and electromagnetic forces and the simplest structural unit displaying the characteristic physical and chemical properties of a compound."

> "Autonomy - the self-governing state or condition of being self governing."

> "Nucleus - mass of gray matter in the brain, where nerve fibers connect. - a positively charged central region of an atom, made up of protons and neutrons and containing almost all of the mass of an atom."

"**Natural Man** - the self-governing central region of an atom, made of protons and neutrons with a stable configuration of atomic nuclei and electrons bound together by electrostatic and electromagnetic forces, containing almost all the mass of atom, and the simplest structural unit displaying the characteristic physical and chemical properties of a compound."

When we say Natural Man, we're talking about the protons, neutrons and electrons bound by electrostatic and electromagnetic forces that hold almost all of the mass atom, while displaying the Character of chemical and physical properties of a compound. This Natural Man has within it, the Spirit MAN that perceives and becomes Conscious as the Soul-of-Man. This is the Life, or Hardcore Reality that lives through it/The Natural Man, as the Governor or Ruler. The Natural Man is the Self and stations of Government which, the Life/Governor/Ruler Governs. Life lives, through the Government of Self. Hence, within the Soul, there is Life; within the Natural Man, there is the Soul that Governs all Natural Motions.

Allow the sample thus far given to unfold as you research the data thus far conveyed. The Hardcore Realist is the Spirit, the Spirit is ALL-MIND; the Soul is its transcendental vehicle of Consciousness, and creation that is able to Reason, Rationalize, construct and discern Thinking from every angle of Feeling and standing; and the Natural Man is the Land, Water, Air and Fire withholding the stations of Government that the Spirit and Soul Governs. These 3 ingredients are really 1 function (BHR 9:29-31). As you read through the chapters and verses of this Book of Hardcore Reality, you'll see this mythology to hold the knowledge of Self-Governing. We will unfold, in our Real Lessons to come, the 3 degree process of how to learn the Science of I AM:

> "After being Raised up by Atom and Evolution, a Natural
> Mother will Nurture your Development in Mass as Spirit.

214

Her Name is called: "Nuhfamuoh•."

- BHR 1:108

According to the Alphabet of Akh-Hulebuk, Nuhfamuoh has various meanings combined into one Thought. There's a Student's way to go about scientifically dissecting its meaning. There's: Nuh-fa-mu-oh. These are 4 sounds. These 4 sounds are the sounds that connect to the Alphabets:

Nuhlē - Fāmah - Mūlē - Māyah

Body – Order – Degree - LWAF

This concept represents the Body. What we will learn about the Body is its order and degrees in connection to the Universal manifest of **L**and, **W**ater, **A**ir and **F**ire (LWAF). **We want to Be clear, that Comprehension is valid regarding Nuhfamuoh not being a planet of some distant time measurement. Nuhfamuoh spells B.O.D.Y.; and it represents your** Bodily - **O**rder - through - **D**egrees - of - **L**and, **W**ater, **A**ir and Fire. **So**

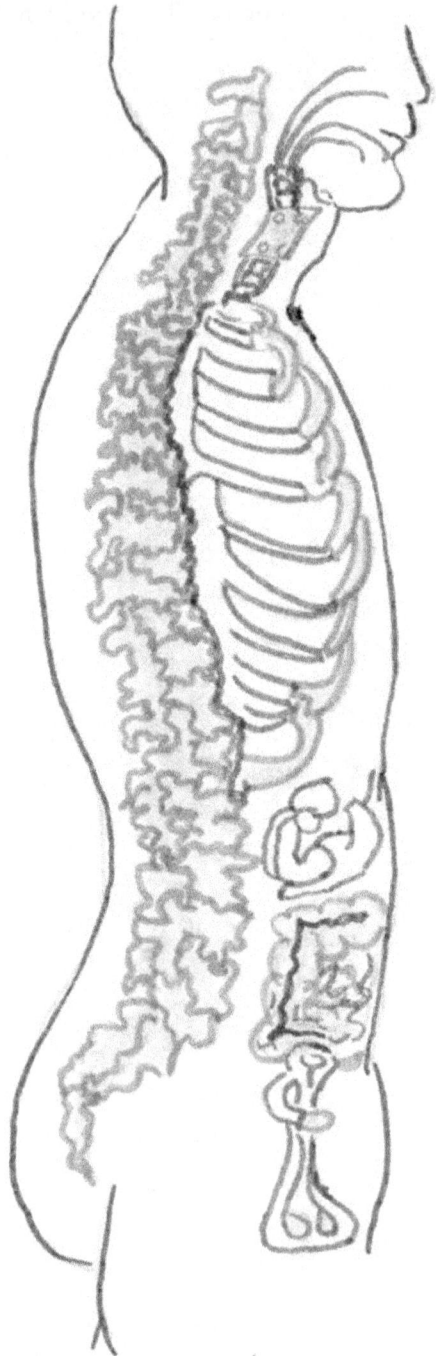

technically, the only planet Nuhfamuoh represents, is your Natural station of Molecules – Autonomy - in a - Nucleus. As the Spirit and Soul within this Planet, you are the Governor that is manifest through the activity of your Conscious Thinking. **All Galaxies – Ozones – Dimensions – and - Stars within yours' and my perceptual sight, are the Youniversal Realities we bring into manifest -via- Nuhfamuoh.** The Body is - in this concept, a Mother, giving Birth to you - the Light of the WORD. So, as we begin bringing Life to the Book of Hardcore Reality, know that the entire Student degree surrounds the arrangement of Comprehending Governing Self. So what we will strongly cover in a Students degree of Learning, in conjunction with Linguistics, Psychometric Mathematics, and the Book of Hardcore Reality itself, is Physiology, Astrology, Earth Science and Sociology. Prepare for major work as this curriculum is designed to distribute.

> "Nuh = Body - The entire material structure and substance of an organism, especially of a Human Being or an animal."

> "Fa = Order - Systematic arrangement and design."

> "Mu = Degree - one of a series of Steps or stages in a process, course of action, progression, or retrogression."

> "Oh = Land - Soil, ground or soil."

>> = Water - any of the liquids passed out of, or in the body.

>> = Air - Breath: Respiration.

>> = Fire - A rapid, persistent chemical reaction that releases heat and light, especially the exothermic

217

combination of a combustible substance with oxygen."

"Nuhfamuoh/ • ⌐ ⊣ ⊃ ⊢ = The entire structured organism of human material, systematically arranged in solids, liquids, Breath and rapid persistent chemical reactions that releases Heat and Light in a series of steps or stages." Accordingly, Nuhfamuoh represents the entire material structure of the Human organisms systematic arrangement of solid, liquid Breath and chemical reactions within it all, releasing heat and light. We learned to discern this systematic arrangement, in steps and stages of progression.

Being that Nuhfamuoh is the Natural Mother, we are her Natural People when we Comprehend the Intelligence-Science-Law-Architecture-and-Mathematics of hers' and our connection. A Natural Person is the flesh and blood living Human Being; the Traveling MAN manifested in flesh. The Natural Person is the SUN of the Natural Mother; it is the Light of the WORD integrated into Nature: the Natural Mother, with GOD-Consciousness; it is the Mind and Soul within the flesh and blood of molecules, Autonomy and a Nucleus. Our intentions regarding this portion of Sample Lesson are to get the potential Student, to stop looking outside of Self, and look within for the Light of the WORD. There's much we don't know about Self. Remember that conditioning and academic "training" has been forced upon generations of us. All of this Time, we've been "trained" to see, and seek Balance outside of our very own Nature. Consider that such may be the very basis of our inability to acutely function through productivity as Human Beings. Balance, is Order. **To find the Balance of Human Standards, we must look within our very own Nature, and study the pattern of the Inner Infrastructure – Symbolism - Labor of – Ancestral - Morale.** As Humans, always know that the Ancients are the Equational Solutions; the

Elements, the Universe and the Grand Order of Divine Service, they are our Ancestry.

The start to Self Governing is Knowing the Inner Infrastructure – Symbolism – Labor – of – Ancestral - Morale. We must first learn the stations in the Natural Person's environment. Nuhfamuoh is Built up through the structures of Land, Water, Air and Fire. From these 4 Structures come the 1+11.2 stations of 7 Hills (BHR 7:51). As Students, we Travel this Journey together as Intelligent Scientists, that must Learn the Way of Nature's Laws and Architectural Mathematical calculations of our Gaining – Obtaining - Developing Balance.

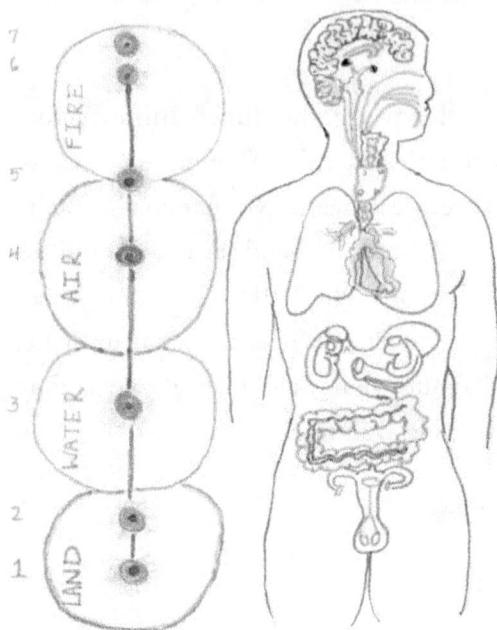

1+11.2 Stations

1.   Integumentary System

2.   Skeletal System

3.   Muscular System

4.   Nervous System

5.   Endocrine System

    6.   Cardiovascular System

7.   Lymphatic System

8.   Respiratory System

9.   Digestive System

10. Urinary System

11. Reproductive System

12. All 11 Systems together as 1 (11+1)

All stations together as 1 functioning unit are in a Balanced Motion ~ via ~ a contraction and expansion called inhale and exhale (1+11.2 = inhale and exhale).

Land	Water	Air	Fire
Reproductive Sys.	Endocrine Sys.	RespiratorySys.	Nervous Sys.
Integumentary Sys.	Urinary Sys.	Cardiovascular Sys.	
Skeletal Sys.	Lymphatic Sys.		
Muscular Sys.	Digestive Sys.		

The beginning process to learning the environment of the Natural Person, is to have an order of arrangement in the /of the Governmental Stations. This chart partionately details the stations according to their alignment with the Elemental structures. They All work together as 1; as we will learn in our Real Lessons.

1 = 11.2 Stations defined

1.   Integumentary - The skin and structures derived from it, such as hair, nails, sweat and oil glands, [function: helps regulate body temperature, protects the body, eliminates wastes, synthesizes Vitamin D and receives certain stimuli such as temperature, pressure and pain.]

2.   Skeletal - All the bones of the body, their associated cartilages and the joints of the body, [function: supports and protects the body, provides leverage, houses cells that produce blood cells and stores minerals.]

3.   Muscular - specifically refers to skeletal muscle tissue; other muscle tissues include visceral and cardiac, [function: participates in bringing about movement, maintains posture and produces heat.]

4.   Nervous - Brain, spinal cord, nerves and sense organs such as the

eyes and ears, [function: regulates body activities through nerve impulses.]

5. Endocrine - All glands that produce hormones [function: regulates body activities through hormones transported by the cardiovascular system.]

6. Cardiovascular - Blood, heart and blood vessels, [function: distributes oxygen, nutrients to cells, carries carbon dioxide and wastes from cells, maintains the acid base balance of the body, protects against disease, prevents hemorrhage by forming blood clots, and helps regulate body temperature.]

7. Lymphatic - Lymph, lymphatic vessels and structures or organs containing lymphatic tissue (large numbers of white blood cells called lymphocytes) such as the spleen, thymus gland, lymph nodes and tonsils, [function: returns proteins and plasma to the cardiovascular system, transports fats from the gastrointestinal tract to the cardiovascular system, filters body fluid, produces white blood cells and protects against disease.]

8. Respiratory - the lungs and a series of associated passageways leading into and out of them, [function: supplies oxygen, eliminates carbon dioxide, and helps regulate the acid-base balance of the body]

9. Digestive - A long tube called the gastrointestinal (GI) tract and associated organs such as salivary glands, liver, gall bladder and pancreas, [function: performs the physical and chemical breakdown and absorption of food for use by cells and eliminates solids and other wastes.]

10. Urinary - Organs that produce, collect and eliminate urine, [functions: regulates the chemical composition of blood, eliminates

wastes, regulates fluid and electrolyte balance and volume, and helps maintain the acid-base balance of the body.]

11. Reproductive - Organs (testes and ovaries) that produce reproductive cells (sperm and ova) and other organs that transport and store reproductive cells, [function: reproduces the organism.]

12. Body - the 11 stations all functioning together as 1 balanced entity through the inhale and exhale, [function: provides the Light of the WORD with an environment to Govern, protect and function in and through.]

7 Hills

In the Students degree, we will Be covering the various meanings to the 7 Hills. At this Sample level, we want to cover the 7 Hills of Law, of Physiology, Life Process and Ancestry. As we advance in the Comprehension of self, the 7 Hills will begin to translate into something more structural and orderly.

We want to be sure that we give you the charts for your research, study and defining for your immediate Comprehension. This way, when we get into our Lesson Books, you will have Comprehension of what we are discussing, Building and learning.

Law	Physiology
1. Mentalism	7. Pineal Gland
2. Correspondence	6. Pituitary Gland
3. Vibration	5. Thyroid Gland
4. Polarity	4. Thymus Gland
5. Rhythm	3. Adrenal Gland
6. Cause & Effect	2. Pancreas Gland
7. Gender	1. Gonad Gland

Life Process	Ancestry
1. Metabolism	1. Proton
2. Excitability	2. Neutron
3. Conductivity	3. Electron
4. Contractility	4. Weak Nuclear Force
5. Growth	5. Strong Nuclear Force
6. Differentiation	6. Electromagnetism
7. Reproduction	7. Gravity

The Reality of this is its structural and functional relation to our very Nature. It is our immediate responsibility to learn the Structural and functional ways of these 7 Hills, to Build up our Character to Comprehend the Circumstances of our existence and the progression therein. Decision making will change if we change our intake of data, and utilize our standings for Balance (BHR 6:13).

GUBAHU

SPIRIT
Territory 3
1 Quarter 7
Buheleh-yahlu

2 Quarter 12

HUMAN
Territory 2
Ehkeahbu

3 Quarter 5

4 Quarter 9
ANIMAL
Territory 1
Ahkeahbuk

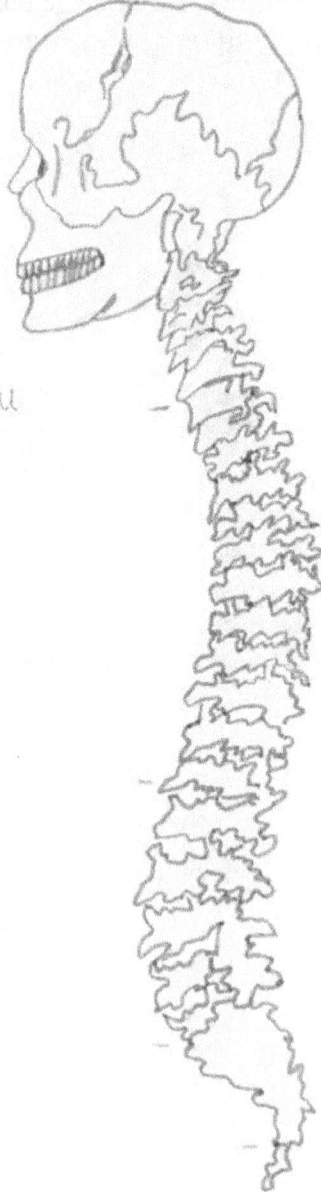

In this portion of the sample, we're showing you what the Road Gubahu is. According to the Alphabet of Akh-Hulebuk•, this is a process of putting sounds together that translates into a Thought and meaning. Gu = **V**, Ba = **S**, Hu = **C**. What we have here, is VSC for Gubahu. VSC is the acronym for **Vertebra of the Spinal Column**. Learning our inner environment, we find that the Road paved in Nuhfamuoh is the Vertebra of the Spinal Column. There are 33 Vertebra in 4 Quarters that have certain meanings (BHR 8:16-27). In the 1st Quarter, there are 7 Cervical columns.

In the 2nd Quarter, there are 12 Thoracic columns. In the 3rd Quarter, there are 5 Lumbar columns and in the 4th Quarter there's 5 Sacral columns and 4 Coccyx columns.

"**Gubahu** - The adult vertebra column enclosing and protecting the spinal cord, supports the head and serves as a point of attachment for the ribs and the muscles of the back. 7 Cervical vertebra in the neck region; 12 Thoracic vertebra in the chest, 5 Lumbar vertebra in the lower back, 5 Sacral vertebra and 4 Coccygeal vertebra making 33 total."

As you will learn, we are the Spirit MAN, that Build up, Travel through and Governs this Natural Man. 33 columns of Pavement has Built around it, the many stations of Nuhfamuoh that we will learn and be in position to Govern.

When we learn to study the Building of Gubahu's columns of Pavement, we will Be entering the 3 stages of development:

1. The centrum body of the vertebra
2. The vertebral arch
3. The 7 Processes of the vertebral arch.

When we better Comprehend this, we'll better Comprehend our inner environment.

As you read the Book of Hardcore Reality, keep in Thought, that this is a curriculum of Self-Knowledge. Although told in a mythological story that seems to skip time spans, **this myth is carefully and strategically composed to lead All initiates into learning about their/our very own Inner being, and how to Become One with it in the Authoritative measurement of time.** As you prepare from this Sample level, learn and study all that you can regarding the Road called Gubahu, and its connection to the Elements, Youniversal Laws, the 7 Hills and our Ancestry. The thing we want for you is to learn how to put all of the data together and make sense of your existence. Chapter 8 in the Book of Hardcore Reality will help you do just that.

Another significant portion of study we will cover in our Student degree, is what the Grand Mother Lodge is. A vertex is the highest point reachable by the initiate in any spiritual disciplines education. This is not to be taken literally. The vertex is also the point where angles align and connect. It is a balance station within, bringing order to Nuhfamuoh. The highest point reachable for a Student to Comprehend, is the heart. The station that we must Travel through for initiation into ISLAM is this Grand Mother Lodge. When we hear People say that the nearest place to meet with any Universal force is in the heart, this means a variety of things. Before going into any Adept or Master teachings, we'd have to travel through the Cardiovascular and Respiratory systems to see the arrangement of this base of balance that allows other systems to connect to its rhythm and function in unison. The Sounds are utilized to construct Ahbuk-Rakebuk; we have Ah = A, buk = L - Ra = G, Ke = M, Buk = L. This is the acronym for ALLAH'S LIGHT in the Grand Mother Lodge. The Light of the WORD, gives Birth to the Rhythmic Pulse tic within the Heart through what we'll learn as the Sinoatrial Node or Pace Setter found on the Superior Vena Cava. We'll also learn how to utilize the Compass and the Square, when penetrating the Lubukmah, Lu = T, buk = L, Mah = W - Three Layered Walls:

The Wall of Lehe - Le = E, he = p - ep = Epicardium 1.

The Wall of Keoh - Ke = M, oh = Y - my = myocardium 2.

The Wall of Lemu - Le = E, mu = d - ed = Endocardium 3.

This will give us a better Inner perception of our highest point reachable as Students and why (BHR 8:43-67).

> "Your station O Executive Rule is at the vertex of Nuhfamuoh. Your Rule of Administration is in fact the center point and Heart of the Land. This Order of Executive Rule is the Sword, and the Administration of enforcement of Law. Enforcement of Law is the Sword's sharp edges."
>
> BHR 9:85

THE GRAND MOTHER LODGE

AHBUK-RAKEBUK

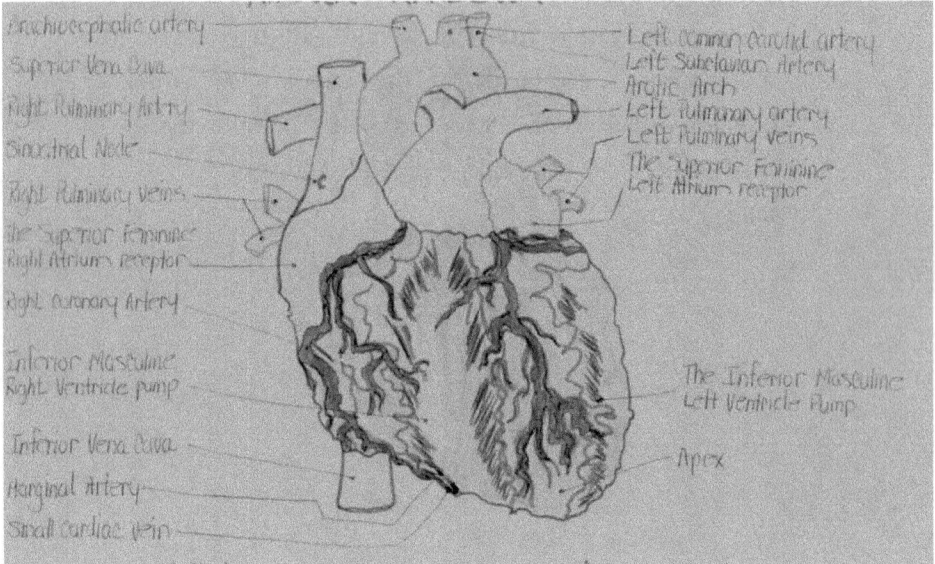

Within us, there are 3 Branches of Government that we will cover. At this level, the Heart is the Executive Branch of Government where we as the Light of the WORD enforce All-Law through this Generating Power. As we cover the grounds and Walls of Ahbuk-Rakebuk, we'll learn how this Governmental Station is the Generator of Rhythm in our Natural Positions.

In the end, we hope that you will support our cause of constructing a Real Education for our youth. This sample version of Lessons is just a brief look into some of the many things that the Book of Hardcore Reality details and we will cover in our Lesson Books to come. We mainly wanted to touch on the Physiological outlook of this Book above all else in this Sample Order, to give All potential Students a starting point in research, study and deciphering the Book of Hardcore Reality. It covers every necessary angle in subject matters our youth and we, generationally have lost sense of. As the perceptual outlook advances, we'll begin to become a collective People again, in Thought, Reason, logic and decision making; more socially and spiritually sound to give constructive and productive direction to our youth when dealing in a fiction surrounding as a Realist.

Remember that I AM a Hardcore Realist. My job is to contribute my perception of acquiring a Real Education, to All who are seeking and searching for answers from a Realist perspective. If you'd like to learn more, or have any input to further this cause, you can write directly to me. If you are interested in the Fall Back Movement and our intentions of helping to uplift the youth with Reality and Truth, then contact Labron C. Neal Bey©™.

Contact me via mail at:

> Andrell Paraham Bey©™ #K81486
> Stateville C.C.
> P.O. Box 112
> Joilet, IL 60434

If this address changes, find me on inmate http://www.search.com at: Andrell Parham #K81486

Contact Labron Neal Bey©™ via mail at:

> Labron C. Neal Bey©™ #B80805
> Stateville C.C.
> P.O. Box 112
> Joilet, IL 60434

If this address changes, find him on inmate http://www.search.com at Labron Neal #B80805

Be a Hardcore Realist, and FALL BACK from the folly and fiction into the Cultivation of I AM.

PEACE & LOVE

REAL SCIENCE
THE CREED OF THE
HARDCORE REALIST

4th Floor metaphor,
climb a 3-step ladder to enter the door
to see All Light with my physical eyes closed,
then open my physical eyes and see darkness infecting the poor,
Character to Comprehend the Circumstances of war,
to correct the Math of this issue is what I live for,
with Science that establishes Mental richness of MIND,
a service to uplift my Kind, Law of the Grand Order Divine,
in a balanced measurement of Time, the People of
Nuhfamuoh will embrace the Intellectualism of The GOD,
through Square standings in Consciousness they will see,
that the amalgamation of Thought and Action
manifests the Creative Energy through the WORD "BE"!
Constructs all Square Standings in GOD Degree, Real Science!
I'm a Hardcore Realist by creed,
I Self Divine, Will be the Unlimited incline the People need
to rise above the illusions of metaphors in materialism,
crush imperialism with ISLAMISM, Supreme Rhythm,
moving fast in a fast pace place
bring Love, Truth, PEACE, Freedom and Justice to the Human race,
erase all incorrect Mathematical hate,
expand a Supreme meditating state, destroy a mental crime rate.
I'll give Solomon's Jewels back, to Queens and Kings
and All illustrious things, Rulership belongs to the GODS,

360° of Intelligent Science poured down from the Highest
Book of Hardcore Reality defeats the odds,
and brings a graduation from darkness to illumination,
psychological tribulations and trials explaining Revelations,
my reputation is firm in representation of ALLAH'S Glory,
Hardcore and Real Story, ordained to give acute prophecy,
Imhotep Will Be my Legacy, decoder of Ancient Masonry,
no longer does Hardcore Reality have to be a Mystery because
the Great I AM is what I AM, a General of Order and Divinity!
I AM; the Light of the WORD on the Rise,
the Hardcore Realist Born as all ignorance dies,
existence Squared in Supreme Perfection,
I Self Law AM; the Resurrection,
example of experience in mental discombobulation, former
victim of imperialism after infiltration,
mental poison was injected into my memory bank and,
it was a distorted, metaphoric, materialistic mess
digested to exploit stupidity, ignorance and foolishness!
Once lost in death but now Raised from the dead,
a Supreme symbolic Rhythm crushing imperialism with ISLAMISM,
Genesis in Mind, Victory shall Be mine, I Self Divine
the unlimited incline my People need,
Off of my Sacrificial Service I intend for them to feed
strong genes from Solomon's seed, this is Real Science!
And I'm a Hardcore Realist by creed!!

STUDENT GOD DEGREES

1. Your standings are upright as you can see straight ahead.

   I AM; the **Student initiate**, standing on the Atlas, Traveling the Journey to the 7th Hill.

2. As you Journey, how do you Focus your sight?

   I AM, the Light of the WORD; this is a GOD Focus where I can see the Light with my 2 physical eyes closed.

3. Do you always Travel your Journey with your 2 physical eyes closed?

   Through the Motion of the WORD'S Light, I AM; the Guided Reality into Equilibrant Form.

4. On your Journey in GOD Focus, are you sure of your destination?

   I stand on my Square within a Circle.

5. Are you traveling your Journey with Direction?

   My Inner, Over and Under standings directs the path of my Outer-standing.

6. What is your degree?

   I AM; a Student in the green.

7. Are you Building a Shelter on your Journey?

   I AM; the Seed of Solomon from the Akh-Hulebuk Carpenters Guild and Born the Light of the WORD through Nuhfamuoh the Natural Mother.

8. You are what you Think. Who are you?

I AM; Pure Infinity of Hardcore Reality; Kebuk - The Son of my Mother; the Light of the WORD and Microcosm of THE ALL.

9. You are what you Think. What are you?

I AM; the 3 that makes 1 called MAN; an **Infinite – Divine – Duality – Hue – MAN - being. I AM** Intelligence – **Science** – Law – **A**rchitecture - **M**athematics; I AM A Hardcore Realist; the Great I AM is what I AM; ALLAH.

10.   You are what you Think. Where are you?

I AM; Ma-SUN/Mason; the manifest of ALL through the Consciousness of the Present Moment; I AM everywhere in Everything, while nowhere in the illusion of everything and nothing in a Time measurement.

11.   You are what you Think. When are you?

I AM; Eternal; the Forever of never ending; the Beginning and the Ending.

12. You are what you Think. Why are you?

I AM; the Balanced Order that comes out of Chaos; the Service to uplift the Consciousness of All Human Individuals.

13. You are what you Think. How are you?

I AM; the Microcosm of the Macrocosmic ALL.

"And Solomon said unto her: "Mahle - child of my wealth, the most valuable jewel from my treasure chest is GOD degree. I AM, the Soul-of-MAN. The Soul is the Consciousness of the Present Moment, capable of Comprehending the Circumstances of Hardcore Reality."

BHR 5:33

I S L A M

Student 1°

I AM, THE WAY Learned,
The Sacred Halls are my Fruit Tree'
Knowledge of Self is my Labor,
To this degree of Masonry I extend Loyalty,
To Build up Nuhfamuoh with this Carpentry;
From The Mothers Nourishment do I feed,
To Be an upstanding part of the Human Family
And a Hardcore Realist by Creed.

Adept 2°

I AM, THE TRUTH Discerned,
Sacrificial service is what I give,
To Teach The People that we can't live LIFE
Because Life within us lives.
I bring Life to the Akh-Hulebuk Carpenters,
Through the Womb – of – MAN's Evolution I
advance;
I show I AM the Reality of ALLAH and ISLAM
In a 720° Geometric stance.

Noble Master 3°

I AM, THE LIGHT Served,
Master Builder with my Tools,
Born The Sun of my Mother
To construct Youniversities, Lodges and Schools.
I AM, the Divine Seed of Solomon;
The Light of the WORD Traveling in a glare,
Geometrically enclosed within a Circle,
Standing as a living perpendicular on the Square.

The Evolution Of The God   In Self

LET'S LEARN A FEW THINGS ABOUT THE AUTHOR

This book is the absorbing theory in vision of the dynamic Andrell Jason Parham Bey©™. "Dre" as we call him, gave us the inspirational ingredients for change. The Book of Hardcore Reality is indeed a high profile, while spiritually calculating, body of work to which we should all behold. The data shows us all who Andrell Jason Parham Bey©™©™ is today, as he consistently studies, learns, evolves and expresses his **I**ntelligence of **S**cience **L**aw **A**rchitecture and **M**athematics for all to learn from and have insight into.

When I first met Dre, he was a young teenage male - the consanguine nephew of my husband, Frederick Parham. "Skeet" - as he is well known by all who love him, diligently worked with Dre in that time, teaching him about the Realities of Life. Being a troubled young Man then, Dre lacked balance, exuded self-confidence and had trouble identifying with what was Real. Although he'd made very bad decisions in his youth, he was a bright and very talented young Man. As I came to know and love him, I realized that he was capable of accomplishing anything he'd put his strong mind to. Unfortunately, he chose the streets and all influences of chaos. There was subsequent trouble, disaster and loss that followed and was inescapable. As a result of his bad decision making, Dre found himself incarcerated for a very long prison term in the Illinois Department of Corrections.

In the beginning stages of his incarceration, things were very difficult for him. I would imagine that it is hard for anyone to adjust to the hell he describes prison to be. He explained that there must be extreme levels of strength exercised to stay focused and not go crazy. With us all working with him, he adjusted and focused in for instruction.

From the beginning, Skeet and I stressed to Dre the significance of education, Manhood, individualism and independence coupled with the idea of applying all studies into the Realities of his existence. Minister Anna Parham - his Mom, stressed the significance of spirituality, principle and faith in conjunction with everything we stressed. Together, we supported - and still do support him, while watching him blossom into the prestigious teacher and servant he is still learning to become.

One of the most prominent attributes displayed through Dre's development was his zeal to learn and know self, as this became a proportionate basis of his educational quest. There came the confidence and maturity of Love for himself.

Love for himself, began to translate through his intentions; and he then wanted all to learn what he was learning. As he began to master the Art of Writing, he started expressing the importance of Knowing and learning Self through the art of poetry, novelty and essay. Seeing that the messages were hard to promote in those specific fields of writing, he readjusted his plans. Informing me of his vision, I encouraged him to stay consistent and relentless in his labor of writing educational data, geared towards helping to save our youth from the rising problems currently facing them. His vision surrounded the blessing of going through hell, surviving the many complications experienced physically, psychologically, spiritually, socially and emotionally, and being given the gift of writing to testify change being attainable even under the most trying and complicated circumstances. Education of what is Real was his goal.

Uniquely, the stars aligned, and Skeet opened the Educational chambers

242

up to "The Hardcore Realist" of which Dre became a faithful Student. The concepts learned coupled with the all of his educational voyage, created the beginning base of the Book of Hardcore Reality. The Cultivation of I AM became the finished product of his labors through the Hardcore Realist Chambers. There is hope that youth in particular, adopts the Hardcore Realist Spirit, so that they will not have to experience the mistakes Dre made in his past, leading to his current incarceration. Continuing to witness the dynamic transition in him, I've been blessed to assist him in the building up of the Book of Hardcore Reality entitled, The Cultivation of I AM – A Know Thyself Curriculum.

As known by all who love him, Dre was born and raised on the South Side of Chicago in the Morgan Park area. An official and authentic Chicago native, he is deeply moved and affected by the chaotic conditions. His passion is in bringing a contributory solution that can and will catch on to the youth. Finding his way outside of his Christian upbringing, he has dug into the Ancient systems of instruction and pulled out ISLAM. A Moorish Scientist, and Moorish American National by birthright, he stands firm on the idea of allowing the Principles of Love, Truth, Peace, Freedom and Justice to be the guiding value system of constructing a contribution of Order. He explains the "old" time religion as Man learning Nature's Laws, learning how we are a part of Nature's Laws, learning cosmic structure and incorporating all that we learn into our Humanity. He explains the ISLAM of this venue as educational and not religious, as religion is practiced today, and recognized in an unbalanced society. ISLAM is the degree rising, learning practice in: Intelligence Science Law Architecture - Mathematics which Dre describes as PEACE: Productive – Education – Activating – Cosmic - Energy. With this Ancient idea of education, the Cultivation of I AM — Book of Hardcore Reality was assembled as an introduction to the leading Mind and Thoughts of Andrell Jason Parham Bey©™©™.

As you read this material, review it with an opened mind to Dre's vision. It is his sincere hope and wish that you will begin to learn who he is, both as a Moorish American National, and Student, Teacher and Servant. I trust that this powerful and inspirational material will have the desired effect on your Conscience, which is to wake up the youth with Hardcore and Real Truth. As an Anthropologist, Moorish Scientist, Director of Education in the Fall Back Movement, Human Being, Father, Uncle, Son, Nephew, and author, Dre strongly believes in the power of Words; and he knows from his personal experiences that they can bring transformation into living. His very existence and its varying degrees of metamorphosis and illumination, confirms how one can claim and evolutionize ones own Divine path. I AM thankful that he's allowed me to tell this small portion of his story.

In closing, I will quote Dre directly:

> "Noble Drew Ali taught, that changing the People comes with a change of literature. I don't want to Build anything from already made structures, because people have their already made theories regarding those bases, and argument and debate emerges from differences in perception unnecessarily. So what I have done, Auntie, is structure a new mythology from old time concepts. I hope that People learn from this, how to face their Circumstances, and say to this artificial world: 'The Great I AM is what I AM.' "

Be Blessed,

Gardenia L. Parham

"Words are the molders of Thoughts; Thoughts are the

molders of activities. There's a power in putting Words together to encourage a particular Order in Activities that will bring Balance to a set of unbalanced Circumstances. We are all responsible for learning how to utilize the Power of Words, to mold the Thoughts that will mold the activities of making contributions of Order into society at large, that the People can have something of worth to utilize in their cause of Gaining Obtaining Developing Character to Comprehend their Circumstances. This is Being Real; I'm a Hardcore Realist!"

Sheik Andrell Parham Bey©™

NOTES

248

NOTES

www.ingramcontent.com/pod-product-compliance
Lightning Source LLC
LaVergne TN
LVHW051254080426
835509LV00020B/2961